# HIGHGROVE

# H.R.H. THE PRINCE OF WALES
# HIGHGROVE

## A GARDEN CELEBRATED

## BUNNY GUINNESS

PHOTOGRAPHY BY
Marianne Majerus,
Andrew Butler and Andrew Lawson

WEIDENFELD & NICOLSON

# CONTENTS

# INTRODUCTION

I FIND IT HARD TO BELIEVE THAT BY THE TIME this book is published I shall have been at Highgrove for 34 years. During that time I have tried to enhance the landscape and the setting of the house; I have tried to create a structure and a framework through the judicious use of hedges, avenues and topiary. Half the battle about making a garden is to ensure there is something interesting to look at in the Winter months, so geometrical shapes and patterns help a great deal – particularly when viewed from the windows of the house. Long shadows cast by avenues and hedges in the Winter sun are, to my mind, an essential, rewarding feature of a garden set in its landscape.

I suppose, when I think about it, I have gardened to a certain extent from a painter's perspective. Each part of the garden is a separate 'painting' and the result of ceaseless walking, ruminating and observing those moments of magic when the light becomes almost dreamlike in its illuminating intensity. It is in those moments when you are lost in wonder that such beauty is possible and inspiration can come in terms of the positioning of new plantings of trees, shrubs and flowers or, for that matter, of architectural features that catch the eye.

I think I learnt quite quickly that placing anything in a garden can easily go wrong if you rush at it, so I have tried never to force a plan or design, but to wait for an 'intuitive' idea to form itself when the moment is right. I have found this of particular value when agonising over where to place pieces of sculpture, for instance. I have been most fortunate over the years to have been given all sorts of things by a succession of generous individuals, organisations, societies, craftsmen and sculptors and it has often taken several years before their correct setting dawned on me.

It is perhaps important, too, to note that much of the garden is the result of my interest in, and patronage of, a whole host of different organisations that have so kindly responded to my particular enthusiasms or desire to protect endangered varieties of plant, vegetable, fruit, tree, shrub or farm animal. It is worth stressing that I found myself growing up at a time when so much that had been carefully and lovingly developed, bred, nurtured and improved over thousands of years of trial and error was being callously and rashly discarded. Thank God there were various far-sighted people in this country who had taken the trouble to set up organisations to try to save something from this carnage of fashionable vandalism. Now, of course, people are beginning to realise that all these things have an intrinsic value and are crucial to our long-term survival. So it has been with the mutual help and support of these organisations and individuals that my garden has taken shape, whether in the establishment of orchards of rare varieties of apple, in the planting of increasingly rare heritage varieties of vegetable, in the development of wildflower meadows and the national collection of beeches and hostas, or in the preservation of critically endangered breeds of farm animals.

In many ways, the garden at Highgrove represents one very small attempt to heal the appallingly short-sighted damage done to the soil, the landscape and to our own souls. Some may not like it, others may scoff that it is not in the 'real world' or is merely an expensive indulgence. Whatever the case, my enduring hope is that those who visit the garden may find something to inspire, excite, fascinate or soothe them.

Snowdrop
*Galanthus nivalis*

# JANUARY

'Everything has gone into suspended animation at this time of year. All of the colour has been drained out of the garden and landscape and little is stirring. A good time to lay hedges, thin out trees in the Arboretum which have grown too close together and plant new trees (if the ground isn't frozen solid). I am a great believer in planting two or three trees in exchange for one taken out. If we are lucky, there may be the odd snowdrop beginning to make an appearance in the Stumpery …'

BELOW The golden yew forms are striking all year round but are at their finest embellished with snow in the Winter.

RIGHT The blush-pink gates flanked by russet walls add warmth to a chilly Winter view of the Kitchen Garden.

THERE IS OFTEN A FRESH CRISPNESS IN January that makes you want to go outside and start moving; the view from Highgrove's tall windows is added encouragement as it offers a promise of colour and life in an otherwise dull season.

In a month when much of the garden is dormant, Highgrove's Kitchen Garden is still a vital and productive place. Here, activity levels are high and regular forays are made to harvest the Winter brassicas, herbs and leeks that fill the geometrically arranged beds. This functional garden looks beautiful at this time of year, as the low Winter light bathes the meticulously landscaped space and picks out all the three-dimensional elements of the design: the tunnel, the heavily pruned and knobbly apple trees that line the walkways and the elegant, curved arbours. Further on, the Stumpery takes on another guise in Winter, as the Summer foliage dies back to reveal the curving mounds of the extraordinary stumps and the fine green oak temples in the more open clearings. On even the darkest days, a visit to the Lily Pool Garden will lighten the soul, as the water bounces the delicate rays of Winter sun around the space, reflecting the ever-changing atmosphere of January's skies.

# Kitchen Garden

Highgrove's Kitchen Garden is a perfect example of a highly productive but beautifully ornamental walled garden, offering something to see all through the year. From the moment you step through the gate, you find yourself enticed along one of many paths that form the bones to this vital garden. The paths offer a practical and aesthetic function, providing access for gardening and dividing this formal space into a geometric pattern of borders and beds. The garden achieves a vivid three-dimensional element to its design by the introduction of height; the lower tier of vegetables within the beds are punctuated by trained trees, curving tunnels and elegant arbours which, even now, stripped bare of the

fruits and flowers which hung from their framework over the Summer months, are still beautiful and give structure to the space. The old, pink walls finish off the design and trap the warm red evening light within their bricks.

For gardeners and non-gardeners alike, the simple geometric design of this garden has a timeless beauty. The crops are carefully laid out, with parallel rows of leeks, cabbages, Brussels sprouts and winter greens interwoven amongst tunnels clad with apple trees and serried ranks of other fruit trees. Traditionally, walled kitchen gardens were built primarily for the production of fruit and vegetables to feed the occupants of the house, but there is a homeliness and feeling of security that enfolds you once you are within the solid, comforting walls. These walls, punctuated with eye-catching gateways cleverly positioned to provide other focal points along the garden's perimeter, were built primarily to protect the produce from rabbits, deer and other predators, and to shelter the vulnerable crops from drying winds and frosts. The radiator effect of the brick walls, absorbing heat from the sun's rays and then slowly releasing it, means that the temperature inside the Kitchen Garden at Highgrove is frequently higher than that of the surrounding area.

Compared to many great estates, the Kitchen Garden at Highgrove is of a relatively modest size: just under two-thirds of an acre; but in its heyday it would have been expected to feed around eight people all year round. By comparison, the kitchen garden built for Queen Victoria in 1844 at Windsor was initially laid out over 22 acres, before it was extended to a massive 31 acres, which required 150 gardeners to maintain it.

The crops and flowers grown here are intended not only to delight the eye but also to feed the household when His Royal Highness is at home or in London. Here we see history in action, and the plot being used for its original purpose, but with a modern twist, as this garden reflects more than any other at Highgrove The Prince's passion for organic gardening.

Paddy Whiteland, who worked for His Royal Highness for many years as a groom and general factotum, remembered seeing the Kitchen Garden being used for fattening pigs before it was lovingly restored to its original form. But when Prince Charles first saw the space in 1980, he reveals it was in a 'rather dissolute state, with its weather-beaten eighteenth-century brick walls glowing in the afternoon sun. I instantly began to see the possibilities for creating something that had been in the back of my mind for several years – a walled garden containing flowers, fruit and vegetables and clipped box hedges.'

This vision seemed a long way off at the time, however, as before him lay merely a small orchard of long-established fruit trees and an old 'dunking' pool in the centre – which was filled in – and the beautiful brick walls, blighted by a section which had fallen away and needed replacing. Undeterred by what was clearly a mammoth project, Prince Charles called on Lady Mollie Salisbury, a passionate gardener and supporter of the organic movement, and together they spent hours poring over plans which were 'madly ambitious – a kind of miniature Villandry,' Prince Charles admits, 'but I soon found I had to moderate such ambitions in the interests of practicality and economy!'

The traditional design of dividing walled gardens into quarters through the use of paths and including a water feature in the centre (often serving a practical purpose, such as being used as a dunking pool or a well to fill watering cans or water carts) dates back to early Persian gardens. This forms the basis of the garden at Highgrove too. The design proposed, which is still in place today, has two main pathways bisecting the almost square space, both horizontally and vertically. The layouts of the squares are designed to reflect the cross of St George and the triangles of the cross of St Andrew.

The filled-in central pool was also resurrected, with just a few modifications. When it was first installed, the fountain was drained and covered every Winter to protect it from the harsh British frosts, but in fact this protective cover caused the thick, velvety mats of moss that clung to the stone to die off. Because the organic, softer, mossy look was one that Prince Charles enjoyed, and the bees and wasps loved drinking from the moss on the water, it was decided to dispense with the cover and it can now be seen all year round – a fine price worth paying, for a little blemish or two to its structure.

LEFT The simple iron hoops of the arch have almost disappeared as the apple trunks have thickened and become part of the garden architecture.

ABOVE The fountain is no longer covered in the Winter as bees like to drink from the fountain's wet moss.

BELOW The Sundial Garden
bathed in low Winter light.

RIGHT The scallops in the yew
hedge provide a glimpse from both
inside and out of this garden.

## Sundial Garden

The gardens at Highgrove have become an increasing passion of Prince Charles's and he has continually developed the appearance and purpose of these areas over the last 34 years. In this time, some of the gardens have been radically changed, but the layout of the Sundial Garden is one that has largely remained unaltered since Prince Charles first had it constructed.

Although the structure has not changed, the planting has seen dramatic alterations. At its conception, the Sundial Garden was laid out predominantly as a rose garden, filled with soft, pastel colours. This subtle, traditional approach made way for a bolder, more dramatic look when it became a black-and-white garden for a short period. Today it is bursting with a mix of mainly herbaceous plants in strong pinks, blues and purples. As this space proves, Highgrove is in no way a garden frozen in time – quite the reverse – as The Prince's experiments with shades of colour and unusual palettes through plants make the gardens constantly evolving and always fascinating.

The Sundial Garden is south facing, and from the very first, its potential as a glorious suntrap was quickly utilised. It is a space that is very much on view from the house, and this, combined with its bold architectural lines created by beautiful hedging and picturesque gates, is key to making it a much enjoyed and well used part of the garden – even in Winter. On warm January days it is tempting to linger

here and enjoy its light and lines, to admire the frost on the hedges and bold clumps of delicate snowdrops which sit snugly in the strip between the bottom of the box hedges and the raised stone edge.

As with much of the estate, when His Royal Highness first arrived, there was no garden as such in this spot; the seemingly inhospitable space just extended into the park, highly visible from the east and buffeted by the ever-prevalent south-westerly winds. There was a fabulous view of Tetbury Church from here, but due to the lack of structure there was also less privacy. In order to make this part of the garden more secluded, one of the first things planted here was the now world-famous yew hedge. Prince Charles had been influenced by the yew hedge that the late Queen Mother had put in at Sandringham, though he varied his design by incorporating regular fourteen-metre shallow recesses. The hedge was then planted in the Winter of 1982. A windbreak made of woven hurdles was constructed along the hedge to help it establish, and also usefully doubled up as a privacy screen.

Attention was then turned to the rest of the space, which was presented as a blank canvas. This had been one of the main reasons the property had appealed to Prince Charles in the first place. In 1980, His Royal Highness, aged 32, was able to acquire a piece of land on which he could make his mark, and to create a garden tailored

17

ABOVE The frost on crisp Winter mornings enhances the architetural elements and structural planting in this south-facing garden.

RIGHT The thatched tree house, set on slate pillars, has been moved and renovated, now ready for another generation to enjoy.

entirely to his needs and vision. Prince Charles was extremely enthusiastic about such a project and reasoned, 'I suppose I liked the idea of starting from scratch'.

Establishing the layout for this new garden was therefore a priority, 'I just worked out a way to go round the garden … I wanted it to be a journey into different compartments.' One of The Prince's favourite gardens was, and still is, Hidcote (designed by Lawrence Johnston), as its clever divisions create strong spaces that can provide much interest for long periods of the year. This idea had a significant influence on Prince Charles's layout.

Another hugely significant influence on Highgrove's development is 'all the different organisations I have become involved with or become president or patron … all of which I minded hugely about'. Meadows, heritage varieties, conservation, architecture and organic gardening are all subjects he is passionate about and as a result many different organisations have had a substantial impact on his own garden.

The former South Garden took on its current name after the arrival of a fine stone sundial, which provides a focal point in the space. This elegant piece of stonework was given to The Prince and Princess of Wales as a wedding gift from the Duke of Beaufort and the outside staff, gardeners and grooms. It was created by Walter Crang, who was a talented local stone mason. On closer inspection, the seemingly simple piece reveals the craft of the mason: around the rectangular sides, Walter has depicted the four seasons, represented by a snowman for Winter, an umbrella for Spring, a rabbit for Summer and a potato picker for Autumn. Around the edge runs this quote: 'A shadow roundabout my face, the sunny hours of day will trace'.

The installation of the sundial was important for The Prince, as this was the first part of the garden proper to be altered to reflect his vision of Highgrove; its arrival determined the shape of the curved beds, which circle around it, providing softness in an otherwise formal space.

# Stumpery

The Stumpery is an outlandish, otherworldly space and one that looks wonderful in the dead of Winter – stripped to its beautiful, shapely bones. This area, which is rather removed from the house and nearest the road, was one of the last to be developed. It was also one of the coldest and noisiest parts of the estate and extremely frost-prone, making it a difficult site to develop. The original intention was for it to be the home of The Prince's National Collection of Hostas, one of his favourite plants, but plans were revised with the intervention of the Bannermans. Julian and Isabel Bannerman are a strong design team recommended to Prince Charles by his friend Candida Lycett-Green, who had seen the work they had done to their own garden, The Ivy, in Chippenham. As Prince Charles admits, before their arrival at Highgrove, 'the woodland was a bit of a mess', even though The Prince had

started to tackle it at the end of the 80s, when it was full of brambles, nettles and laurel jostling with areas of planting that were struggling to survive.

The canopy of trees was mainly formed by sycamore, larch and beech, with the occasional oak and some balsam poplars planted by Prince Charles. Initially there were many more trees, but a Winter gale in the Eighties caused a dramatic natural thinning. The increase in light levels that resulted was hugely beneficial, however, and enabled Rosemary Verey to help Prince Charles introduce some initial informal planting in what was originally referred to as the Woodland Garden.

Before they could do this, though, they had to tackle the heavy, thick clay. Tons of well-rotted manure was rotavated in before the plants that could tolerate relatively minimal maintenance, such as geraniums, foxgloves, violas, scented

RIGHT The foreground to the Wall
of Gifts is a dappled woodland carpet,
heaving with snowdrops in January.

white tobacco plants and many bulbs were planted. John
Hill, a landscape gardener who worked with Rosemary,
recalls helping The Prince with the planting. 'I remember
working on a scrubby area with The Prince one afternoon.
He was a couple of years older than me, and I had always
considered myself pretty fit, but I was not much of a match
for The Prince. He attacked the site with great gusto and
I was struggling to keep up!'

The original idea for the Stumpery was to create a circle
with three entrances, a layout inspired by The Circus in
Bath. The Bannermans had also been inspired by images of
the spiky, stump-like metal sea defences that the Japanese
use along their coast and various rooteries built in the
eighteenth century, such as the Hermit's Cell (listed II*),
which was built in around 1750 at Badminton House by
Thomas Wright. After discussions with The Prince, it was
agreed that stumps would be the ideal elements to create
evocative, mood-enhancing entrances and boundaries
into the new garden.

There is a spectacular tree house just outside the
original core part of the Stumpery, but now within its
boundaries (the Stumpery was later extended significantly,
as it was so successful, to enable a pool and other elements
to be added). The tree house, or 'Hollyrood House' as it was
called by the designer, Willie Bertram, was built in 1988
when the young Princes William and Harry were aged just
five and three. Willie suggested to The Prince, 'that as it was
for the boys then he might allow me to interview Prince
William to find out what he had in mind?' Prince Charles
agreed and sent William along. At the interview the young
prince said, 'I want it to be as high as possible so I can get
away from everyone and I want a rope ladder which I can
pull up so no one can get at me.'

Thus Hollyrood House was built, complete with holly
leaf-shaped balusters topped by a holly-berry red rail, a
holly leaf-shaped doorway and a thatched roof. It was
positioned in a magnificent holly tree some ten metres
high and was completed just in time for Prince William's
seventh birthday on 21 June 1989. Prince Charles obtained
'royal opening-type' tape, which was ceremoniously cut.

Sadly, about a year and a half later, the tree died from
honey fungus and the whole structure had to be moved
a few metres away to where it stands now, near one of
the temples. It no longer sits in a tree but is supported by

about ten tall hunks of rough-hewn Welsh slate standing
stones, in a design by Stephen Florence. It was re-thatched
by a master thatcher, Matthew Higham, who had first done
it while working there on a Youth Training Scheme. The
holly leaf balustrade has since been replaced by a cleft
oak post-and-rail fence, ready for the next generation
of princes and princesses.

The planting that envelops the Stumpery totally
integrates the structures into the landscape. There is
something particularly wonderful about coming across
flowers, fragrances and berries in mid-Winter, and in the
sheltered confines of the Stumpery, the season's precious
flowers and subtle fragrances are protected from the
harsher Winter gales. In January, hellebores, especially the
Lenten rose (*Helleborus orientalis*), hug the banks in cheery
bunches, bashfully bowing their heads, an etiquette The
Prince has tried to prevent by raising them up the sides
of the banks so their delicate 'faces' are still visible.

Jostling among the hellebores are other Winter favourites including snowdrops, which have formed thick, healthy clumps over the years, and delicate carpets of *Cyclamen coum*. Among these, the variety *C. c.* 'Maurice Dryden' stands out, not just for its traditional white flowers but for the green-edged, pewter-coloured leaves that lie beneath them.

A little extra height is brought into the planting scheme by low 'hedges' of native butcher's broom (*Ruscus aculeatus*), which look spectacular in Winter when speckled with bright red berries. The banks that line the edge of the icy pool in Winter are clothed with Winter heliotrope (*Petasites fragrans*), whose tall, violet-pink flowers appear sporadically but not profusely throughout the season, rising high above heart-shaped leaves, and filling the Stumpery with their soft vanilla scent.

Shrubs play an important part in this scheme too, and the Stumpery is filled with carefully chosen woodland favourites renowned for their sensational scents. The elegant *Viburnum × bodnantense* 'Dawn' is positioned to add height to the scheme; its tall upright stems are stripped bare of leaves in Winter, but the naked branches are instead covered with heavily scented pale pink to white

BELOW The Lenten rose is raised up on the banks, encouraging you to engage with its spectacular colours and markings.

RIGHT The sweet chestnut stumps crown the mounded banks of the Stumpery, which are becoming colonised by mosses and ferns.

blooms. Alongside, the shrubby evergreen Christmas box (*Sarcococca hookeriana*) offers lower-level interest with neat mounds of dark green, glossy, neat leaves. You might be forgiven for not seeing its small, white flowers, but their powerful scent will permeate the glade, making sure you look to discover its source.

In Winter the Stumpery is at its aesthetic and olfactory best, and care is taken even in these months to ensure it stays that way. Routinely now, in late Winter or early Spring, all the extensive planting areas are covered with a heavy dressing of well-decomposed wood and bark mulch, which acts to show off the early-flowering plants and provides an immaculate rich-brown duvet to cosset the intrepid early risers.

Over the years The Prince has worked hard to create the Stumpery's mystical and organic look and feel, and as you wander through the fragrant glade in mid Winter, it is easy to believe that it has been there for ever.

## Column and Avenues

If you stand with your back to the front door of Highgrove House and look almost due north, you see the striking Lime Avenue that runs through the Park, leading towards a fine column. The Lime Avenue was planted here in 1994 to commemorate the twenty-fifth anniversary of Prince Charles as Chairman of The Princes' Council of the Duchy of Cornwall, and was given to him by the members of the council.

The avenue is impressive – stretching over half a kilometre in length – and is particularly striking early on a Winter morning or in the late afternoon when the long, sharp shadows cast by the many trees emphasise the avenue's architectural drama as it slices through the Parkland. John White, the former curator botanist at the renowned Westonbirt Arboretum who helped The Prince design the avenue, saw this spot as, 'a gift of a position for an avenue'. The exact bearing of the avenue is 15 degrees, so the sun shines along its length at about 12.15pm, framed by the two prominent lines of trees, which produces an extraordinary effect that is quite a sight to see.

Lime trees were selected rather than oak or beech (the other candidates) as they are relatively fast-growing and do not get attacked and misshapen by squirrels (as do beech), and oak was dismissed because it is a slow-growing tree. The type of lime, *Tilia platyphyllos* 'Rubra', was selected because it produces little epicormic growth (the characteristic bushy growth that often develops around the base of the trunk), which would distract from the desired effect of the clean stems required to create an avenue of pleached trees.

Many people assume all avenues are planted with pairs of trees opposite each other, but when you walk down this amazing double wall of trees, you probably would not notice that the trees are staggered, or arranged in a herringbone pattern. Trees need light and root space to grow into fine specimens, so by off-setting them they have a greater chance of better health and therefore live longer.

Sixty-seven trees were used to create the avenue, spaced 16 metres apart across the width and between each one. These distances would enable a viewer to see a 12-metre obelisk 1.5 kilometres away after 150 years, provided, of course, the lower branches of the trees were regularly trimmed from the trunks.

To be absolutely sure of this view, sketches were drawn to illustrate the height of the trees and how they would look at 10-, 20-, 30- and 150-year intervals. If planted as small, feathered trees, they would initially be about 5 metres tall, with a 3-metre spread in 10 years' time. At 20 years, they would reach the height of the obelisk; at 30, the top of the obelisk would be out of sight of the house, and from then on, the crowns would need to be lifted to restore the view.

The avenue is not quite 20 years old and so has a while to go until it forms the desired 'wall of wood' effect, expected when it reaches the 100-year mark. Each trunk is surrounded by tree guards that have near-horizontal timbers, which wind round the four corner posts to create an unusual lattice effect.

Walking between the parallel rows of young, bare lime trees, you see the tall column ahead, luring you on.

The column sits atop a dry stone base, which forms a convenient seat to rest and survey the Parkland. It was designed by The Prince and Willie Bertram and was built in 1993, at the start of this project. The splendid, gilded phoenix that stands some 3.5 metres high on top of the column was designed and made by Isabel and Julian Bannerman and was commissioned as a 50th birthday gift to The Prince from the Sultan of Oman. The Prince had asked the Bannermans to design something to finish off the column and they thought a phoenix, which is a sacred, mythical bird associated with the sun, and has the ability to catch fire and be 'reborn' would be an apt choice.

The bird and nest are crafted from gilded metal. It took six months to create and when finally finished, a crane was used to position the phoenix on top of a cast-iron column that was salvaged during the demolition of Victoria Railway Station in London and was given to The Prince by Sir William McAlpine. At the foot of the column a commemorative plaque reads:

*This avenue of lime trees was presented to HRH The Prince of Wales, Duke of Cornwall, in 1994 to celebrate his 25*[th] *anniversary as chairman of The Prince's Council by members of council staff of the Duchy of Cornwall.*

Your attention is also pulled to another avenue, more recently planted than the Lime Avenue, which consists of London plane trees (*Platanus × hispanica*) alternating with tulip trees (*Liriodendron tulipifera*), and leads from the column back to the Orchard Room. This attractive walkway will become even more stunning as it matures and the plane trees develop their characteristic flaking grey and cream patterned bark.

Some existing trees were already growing in the proposed line here when the new planes were planted, so their position has been carefully worked in with the spacing of the newer plane trees – not an easy task, but worth doing to keep these lovely specimens. As ever, conservation is key in a garden that reflects the environmental ethos of its owner.

# Lily Pool Garden

Walking up the Thyme Walk with the sun setting behind the Lime Avenue on a Winter evening, you can see the glow of the low, red sun skimming the water of the Lily Pool. The imposing view of the gladiator, a fine life-size bronze which is a copy of an original (dated about 100 BC) that has an extraordinary history, is set in the space between the two arcs created by the yew hedge. The bronze, given to The Prince by Lord Cholmondeley, is flanked by two massive urns. The unplanted sherry jars that stand proud off the yew hedges were also gifts to Prince Charles, by the owner of the Assisi Garden in Italy, and the story of their arrival has an amusing twist. These fine gifts were sent simply addressed to 'The Prince of Wales, Tetbury' – so the lorry driver had mistakenly dropped them off at the nearby pub, much to the landlord's surprise!

This design is very much the result of Prince Charles's vision. When he arrived at Highgrove, there was a pool in this site, which was, according to The Prince, 'a pretty dreadful square pond with an equally dreadful fluted stone pot in the middle of it'. His Royal Highness was keen to retain a water feature but wanted to make it more exciting, so he contacted William Pye, who is internationally famous for his water-feature creations.

In 1992, Bill Pye visited Highgrove and met his royal client over lunch, who asked him 'to come up with some ideas'. Bill and Willie Bertram then collaborated and together came up with the idea of producing 'a raised table of water' in a curving, cross-shaped form. This 'raised table' envelops a slightly sunken pool built in the shape of a quatrefoil, sitting about 30 centimetres above it. Water continually flows over the four weirs of bronze at the ends of the cross, producing a soothing trickling sound. The beautiful ashlar (York) stone sides that contain this raised body of water are narrow, just over 2.5 centimetres or so wide, and only fractionally higher than the enclosed water body, ensuring the viewer's focus is on the water and its ever-changing reflections. Bill Pye modelled the weirs himself before they were cast in bronze, creating parrot-beak spouts to 'throw' the water in an amazing curved sheet of silver, which at the same time adds another layer to the calming, harmonious sounds within this garden.

The raised design was deliberate in order to enable the water to catch more light and reflections from the sky and surrounding landscape. The outer pool was designed by Willie Bertram, who cleverly made the sides overhanging, which created dark, private niches under the coping for the fish to hide from herons and other predators.

The yew hedging and topiary that surround the Lily Pool create a strong architectural feature, and the longer you look at them, the more you begin to see that the layout of the hedges reflects the position and shape of the original rectangular pool, and so were moved slightly to reinforce the new, curvaceous effect of the new pool.

Two seats were raised up on either side and are backed by curved hedging, which also swoops up and down. Both sides have tall, beautifully sheared swirls of yew. The edge of the yew by the openings is cut with an overhang, mimicking a stone coping. Parts of the hedging here are at a height lower than the main hedge – at just over a metre – which opens up to views of the Meadows and surroundings.

The pool is a happy sight for both resident and visiting birds that appreciate it as a constant, year-round source of accessible water – even in the coldest weather. The almost flush levels allow even the smallest birds to perch on the ashlar lip of the pool and enjoy a drink when everything else around them is frozen.

LEFT The bronze Borghese Gladiator statue is a copy of the original, which is located in the Louvre in Paris.

RIGHT The pool has a high water level, allowing birds to drink from the side, even when it is covered in snow. It also increases its reflective qualities, bouncing Winter light around the garden.

Winter aconite
*Eranthis hyemalis*

# FEBRUARY

'The days are just beginning to lengthen and with the subtle change in light, the Winter silence is broken in the mornings by the most wonderful dawn chorus from the birds outside my window. The chickens, which have refused to lay during the low light levels of the Winter, start once again to produce their gift of dark brown eggs. By now, the various parts of the garden should have been tidied, cut back and given a good mulching from our own homemade compost. In my opinion, well-rotted cow manure – in liberal quantities – is also the secret ingredient for any garden. The darker purple crocuses – which I love – may be starting to show their heads and saffron mouths around the base of the trees, while the hoped-for carpet of pink and purple cyclamen in the Arboretum can help to raise the spirits in anticipation of Spring.'

It is a sad truth that as the cold weather lingers in February, many gardens continue to look bleak and offer no respite to a Winter-weary soul; however, at Highgrove there is an uplifting sense of hope, for this is when many areas begin to break free from their seasonal shackles and burst into life.

In the more wooded gardens, such as the Arboretum and Winterbourne, there are a myriad of bulbs, especially snowdrops, aconites and daffodils, which take advantage of the higher light levels before the leaves on the trees break out and consume it, carpeting the ground with a patchwork of colour in the gloom of Winter. These areas are marginally warmer, too, as they are sheltered and insulated by the dense sylvan canopy, which also helps to nurture the first signs of life. The greenhouse and working areas are abuzz with activity now, as gardeners gear up to furnish the beds and borders in Spring, and sow seed frenetically. The Cottage Garden, in its prime sheltered spot with warm south-facing walls that soak up every bit of sun, creates an ideal area to coax the seasonal bulbs and February flowers to emerge and show themselves off to their best ability.

BELOW This jar (one of a pair) was delivered to the local pub, as it was simply addressed to: The Prince of Wales, Tetbury.

BELOW RIGHT The muted colours of this gateway to the Cottage Garden are original and subtle; they work in bright sunlight but also enliven the palette on dull Winter days.

ABOVE RIGHT Prince Charles enjoys tending to the bird feeders himself. The bird population and diversity has increased dramatically in recent years.

# Cottage Garden

The Cottage Garden is a much-used and much-loved garden which is enjoyed for most of the year, and even before The Prince of Wales moved to Highgrove, this more sheltered part of the garden had been a popular part of the grounds for generations of families.

It is difficult to believe, but most of the garden was, until recent years, extraordinarily exposed. However, as this space is protected from the harsh eastern winds, it has become relatively balmy since The Prince's arrival and subsequent development of the house and gardens. The Cottage Garden is now a space that is about 100 metres long and 20 metres wide, running parallel to the drive and conveniently sited near the route to the stable yard from the house.

In February, it is exciting to wander along the broad serpentine-shaped grass path that meanders through distinct sections. Although the borders are predominantly packed with perennials and annuals, late-Winter-flowering bulbs and shrubs welcome you as you follow the linear garden towards the Meadow. All the wide borders

flanking the walls and buildings here are south facing and additionally enjoy some protection from the light tree canopies above, making it the ideal protective environment for the late-Winter flowerers.

As befits a much-frequented garden, the planting scheme has been carefully planned to ensure there is colour here all through the year – not forgetting Winter. In February the garden is given a vibrant lift by the inclusion of plants such as *Cornus mas*, the cornelian cherry, which grows next to the Indian Gate and bears clusters of single flowers grouped together, each consisting of four pale, sulphur-yellow petals set against naked, greenish twigs. Another favourite is *Lonicera fragrantissima*, the shrubby, semi-evergreen honeysuckle also known as the January jasmine (though it performs for far longer than a month).

The view of the central section of the Cottage Garden is simple but sensational, especially if you enter via the Indian Gate. The graceful, leaning holm oak tree with its generous 'Lord's bench' made of clipped box around its trunk unashamedly takes centre stage. This venerable oak has recently been crown lifted (by which process the lower branches are removed) to allow more light to penetrate and reach the daffodils (*Narcissus* 'Jenny' and 'February Gold') and dark purple crocuses below. Most guests enter the Cottage Garden from the Orchard Room via the Indian Gate. This results in it being less conspicuous from the entrance via the drive, which increases the element of surprise the visitor feels on arrival and somewhat divorces it from the Cotswold landscape.

Entering from the drive brings you first to a solid, simple and generously wide door painted in Highgrove blue/green and hung with ivy. A short stretch of path is flanked by metre-high walls created from randomly placed, generously sized blocks of stone reclaimed from Hereford Cathedral. Passing through, you then arrive at the beautiful carved and studded double doors complete with decorated pillars, which came from Jodhpur in 2006. Prince Charles discovered these doors discarded at the side of the road on one of his foreign tours. He has had them housed under an Asian-inspired building that was built by estate staff and topped with a two-tiered roof of shingles cut from Sandringham oaks.

The Cottage Garden now includes the Mediterranean Garden: a more traditional garden around the new Summerhouse, an area beyond this with deep, island beds and a mulberry tree, a shady section by the holm oak, the

Buttress Garden and a laurel tunnel. These gardens were developed from the strip of land created to the north of one of the long runs of yew hedging.

When the yew hedge was laid out in the mid-Eighties it left a long, thin, unprepossessing strip of ground between the new hedge and the driveway. Prince Charles recognised its potential and decided to contact Rosemary Verey for some more advice. Prince Charles was extremely grateful for her help: 'Her advice, and her genius for finding the right plant to go in the right place, and to provide interest and colour at different times in the year, has proved invaluable,' he remarked.

Rosemary made her first visit to Highgrove shortly after, during which Prince Charles outlined a general plan for his 'cottage garden' including the creation of informal, snaking borders behind the new yew hedging. On the right-hand side there was an existing shrubbery of sorts and also a few large trees dotted throughout, including the fine evergreen oak that remains today and some fastigiate yew.

LEFT *Crocus* 'Remembrance' naturalise well and have white stripes on their green foliage. They bring colour when most around is bare.

ABOVE The Indian Gate has beautifully carved, studded doors, which Prince Charles discovered by the roadside in Jodhpur. Most visitors enter the Cottage Garden via this gate from the Orchard Room.

The 'brief' for the Cottage Garden included traditional cottage plantings of trees, shrubs, many perennials, a few annuals and lots of bulbs. From this, Rosemary drew out the curving borders and detailed the planting within them. There was little of the formality and structure that is often associated with Rosemary's schemes; instead the area was filled with drifts of flowing planting including pots of honesty, *Lunaria annua* 'Purpurea', *Actaea simplex* Atropurpurea Group, *Acanthus mollis*, *Stachys lanata*,

*Penstemon* 'Evelyn', *Lavatera × clementii* 'Barnsley', *Hydrangea arborescens* 'Annabelle', and various delphiniums. Many of these are still firm favourites of Prince Charles today.

By the end of a long day, by which time Rosemary and John Hill, who worked with her, had set out the plants and Prince Charles and Rupert Golby had planted them with the occasional help of the young Princes (Harry, aged four, enjoyed watering though William was not that keen), it was all pretty much done. As the light began to fade, rain obligingly started to fall. Photographs from that year show the embryonic beds edged with randomly shaped pieces of flat stone (as many are today) and it looked very much a family-friendly garden, with children's play equipment scattered across the lawn.

BELOW This stone bench (one of a pair) is flanked by two Grecian urns, planted with *Hydrangea paniculata*.

# Arboretum

One of the immensely satisfying aspects of having a relatively long involvement in a garden, whatever its size, is that dramatic changes can be created over the years. The creator and the garden develop an increasingly strong bond, and there is always more potential and promise to create an ever-more magnificent space and an even better garden. To this end, perhaps the greatest changes at Highgrove have been seen in the Arboretum.

When His Royal Highness first moved to Highgrove, this area, which is about a half of an acre in size, was an unkempt larch plantation that had become a jungle of nettles and scrub. Now when you step through the gates from the Kitchen Garden, having crossed through the Azalea Walk, you enter a wonderful, lightly wooded sheltered area. Even in February there is colour, form and fragrance here, provided by a magnificent lower storey of pink and purple cyclamen (*Cyclamen coum*), a gold-yellow glow from Winter aconites (*Eranthis hyemalis*), and the blue star-shaped flowers of puschkinias (*P. scilloides* var. *libanotica*). The middle storey of smaller trees and large shrubs is mainly made up of deciduous plants, but even some of these are in flower in these late Winter months.

They include the delightful early flowering cherry *Prunus* 'Kursar', with its deep pink saucer-shaped flowers that smother its branches. When its leaves open they are bronze-red initially before turning fresh green.

The Persian ironwood (*Parrotia persica*) is a very fine tree too. One grows in a prime position next to the Sanctuary and now, as January rolls into February, its tiny, spidery, crimson flowers pull you towards this little-known but outstanding tree. It apparently has virtually indestructible timber – hence its common name – but the main reason for growing it is usually its unrivalled Autumnal colour, going from yellow through orange to red.

Less dramatic but welcome contributors to the late Winter scene are some huge, rounded, green box bushes which add a pleasing solidity and colour among the predominantly naked (albeit shapely) stems. There are also large topiary yews near the high, east wall of the Azalea Walk, which are the surviving remnants of an old yew hedge. One or two have developed into beautiful yew trees, others have been transformed into huge, dark green clipped shapes – there is a massive boar's head, a magnificent frog and a squirrel, all striking, life-like and humorous pieces. These and the box bushes are not only beautiful but also, being native plants, provide welcome interest in Winter, shelter from harsh winds and an ideal habitat for small mammals and birds.

The Arboretum is all about stunning plants, but there is an important piece of artwork here too – 'The Daughters of Odessa: Martyrs of Modernism', which stands at the end of the yellow azalea-lined vista as you enter the Arboretum from the middle of the Azalea Walk. This fine bronze was given to His Royal Highness from the United States of America as a 'thank you' to him for his support of arts and architecture. It was presented to The Prince by Frederick Hart, the sculptor, and unveiled in 1997. The 'Daughters' are Anastasia, Tatania, Olga and Maria, the children of Tsar Nicholas II of Russia, who were killed in the Bolshevik Revolution in 1918. They are called 'martyrs' as they represent beautiful qualities which have been rather forgotten in the twenty-first century. 'The ability to have Faith, sustain Hope, feel the transforming power of Beauty and revel in the Innocence around us. Faith, Hope, Innocence and Beauty, the four daughters of Odessa'.

Wrapping part-way around the statue is a beautiful wood bench, which formed part of a garden designed by Stephen Florence for The Chelsea Flower Show, dedicated to Queen Elizabeth the Queen Mother. The bench was later moved to this site.

His Royal Highness has had a keen interest in trees for many years, and wanted someone who could advise him on the Parkland trees, the tree belts on the farm and the individual specimens around the gardens. He was also inspired by the magnificent acer collection next door at Westonbirt Arboretum.

At that time, Paddy Whiteland worked at Highgrove; Prince Charles has said of him, 'Everything I have achieved at Highgrove could not have been achieved without Paddy. He is one of the best and truest of individuals and I am forever indebted to him.'

## Winterbourne Garden

The former Southern Hemisphere Garden (which contained many borderline tender plants from that part of the world) was renamed the Winterbourne Garden in March 2012, and subsequently has been reworked and developed to change the emphasis on the planting. This garden is now a lushly planted space; while some of the existing exotics, such as the Chusan palm (*Trachycarpus fortunei*) and tree ferns have been retained, many hardier shrubs and groundcover have also been added to the scheme. In February, however, it is crocus and daffodils that steal the show.

The dramatic change in planting style was brought about by the harsh Winters of 2010 and 2011, which resulted in a fair few losses here. The story of this area is interesting, reflecting the way gardeners can respond to changes over which they have no control and use them to their advantage.

This space, which is slotted in between the north side of the Kitchen Garden wall and the Meadow, is thought to have originally been used to accommodate the main Bath Road, many, many years ago. When you stroll through this sheltered, lightly wooded area now, there is not a trace of its former life. The high brick wall of the Kitchen Garden forms the boundary along the northern side and the garden runs parallel to it. This dominant wall adds shade, definition and contrast to an otherwise strongly plant-oriented space.

Gardening beside a tall north wall creates huge opportunities – the extremes of temperatures are much reduced by its protection and the quality of the softer light in the space creates a cool atmosphere. His Royal Highness enjoys observing this space under differing light conditions – it can be exceptionally dramatic when it is lit from the west in the evening, when the low, cool light accentuates the differences in planting levels and highlights the three-dimensional character of the scheme.

It was decided back in the mid-Nineties that this sheltered spot offered an exciting opportunity to grow less hardy plants at Highgrove, as the existing large mature trees and thickets of cherry laurel provided protection at a lower level from the easterly winds. The growing of more

Paddy was famous among the locals and knew John White, who was curator at nearby Westonbirt Arboretum, and so introduced him to Prince Charles, in order to share his knowledge on trees. One day when Prince Charles and John White were grubbing out snowberry bushes in this plantation, the two agreed that the area would make an excellent arboretum.

White drew up some proposals that concentrated on using a small number of tree species that would fulfil The Prince's brief to provide bright Spring colour and fiery Autumn shades. To his mind, it is important to focus on trees from particular regions, or on a selected few species, or on trees with particular features – otherwise, if random trees are selected, the hugger-mugger that results does not show off the trees in their best light.

Prince Charles's favourite trees include Japanese acers and cherries, which were good choices for the site. The soil type in the proposed arboretum space is a sandy forest marble to a fantastic depth of 1.5 metres, overlying lime-stone. It is fortuitously acidic (most Japanese maples favour a neutral to acid soil) rather than the more limey soil that is to be found in much of the rest of the Highgrove estate. A final criterion for the agreed brief was conservation, and the Arboretum provided the perfect opportunity to include really interesting specimens, notably some of the National Collection of beech.

unusual, tender plants, including tree ferns and palms, was inspired by some of the more exotic plants and specimens grown at Osborne House on the Isle of Wight. Some of these would be brought back to Highgrove to try in the Southern Hemisphere Garden, such as *Lapageria rosea*, the Chilean box thorn *Vestia foetida,* and *Beschorneria yuccoides*.

The planting still has a strong dramatic element, lending an almost tropical atmosphere, which is enhanced by a charming natural water course. The Winterbourne stream that gives this garden its current name trickles through this space, so-called because it runs in Winter (from the Anglo-Saxon word, *burna*, meaning stream) but dries up most Summers, is a delight. It is a narrow, tranquil length of water that flows at the bottom of a fern-clad ha-ha wall, but as Winter turns into Spring, gunnera (*Gunnera manicata*), primulas, (*Primula florindae, P. pulverulenta* and *P. japonica* 'Miller's Crimson') and the golden, luxuriant marsh marigold (*Caltha palustris*), all of which enjoy this damp sheltered position, burst into life. This part of the garden, above the ha-ha and Winterbourne stream, was created by clearing out a mass of tangled laurels and holly.

Within the garden the use of stone is repeated to subtly echo the man-made walls. Built into the stone-retaining wall that lines the stream are five archways, which look like ornate stone buttresses, interspersed along its length. These fine bits of reclaimed carved masonry came from Hereford Cathedral and their formality contrasts beautifully with the more naked naturalness of the stream. One of the buttresses serves as a bridge, allowing you to step up onto the higher level and investigate the denser, wide and more informal beds of planting that skirt the Meadow. Another surprise is three beautifully made slate pots, the profiles of which contain strong curves. These were made by the sculptor Joe Smith and are formed from horizontal courses of slate (in a similar way to which a dry stone wall is built).

Tree ferns are still prominent in this remodelled garden, although there are fewer now than a few years ago when we enjoyed warmer Winters and hotter Summers. The dominant, hairy trunks are dotted around the space, ranging in height from four metres tall to more diminutive specimens of just 60 centimetres or so. Most of these are

the hardier species of tree fern, *Dicksonia antarctica*, and they lend a striking air to this garden. Sixty were given to Prince Charles for his sixtieth birthday in November 2008, a much-appreciated present from the Monarchist League of Australia. During the Winter period the dramatic fronds are wrapped up in hessian and the crowns packed with straw to protect their vulnerable crowns from frost.

When the Southern Hemisphere Garden was in full swing, the presence of several large specimens of the Chusan palm (*Trachycarpus fortunei*), eucalyptus, phormiums, astelias (*Astelia chathamica*) and lapagerias transported you to another part of the world. Prince Charles referred to this as 'My little bit of exotica in Gloucestershire' and enjoyed, as many keen gardeners do, challenging the scope of what can be grown in our gardens in Britain.

Lenten rose
*Helleborus orientalis*

# MARCH

'If you try to paint landscapes it is during this
month that the light begins to change, almost as
if the sky is beginning to shed its old skin and
take on a sparklingly fresh new one. Down the
front drive, bright throngs of the early narcissi,
'February Gold' and 'Jenny', gladden the heart,
while adventurous daffodils in the Meadow risk
late snowfalls and sudden cold spells and deck
themselves in hesitant yellow sou'westers … In the
Arboretum, the acers I planted some 15 years ago
are inclined to respond too enthusiastically to bouts
of warmer sunshine, only to be threatened with
dire consequences by sharp frosts.'

## Front Drive

THE ARRIVAL OF MARCH BRINGS WITH IT THE anticipation of Spring, and this is reflected throughout the entire garden. The Sundial Garden in particular is starting to look vibrant now; on full view from the house and on a warm Spring day, it can be a soothing place to sit and enjoy the gentle heat of the sun and early scents and blooms in the surrounding borders. A short stroll along the Main and Front Drive allows expansive views across the Meadow where there is a palpable sense of this expanse gathering momentum; the bulbs are bursting through the soil, herbs are filling out and the birds and bees are busy – the latter appearing as soon as there is some warmth in the sun. In the Kitchen Garden, the rows of lettuce, peas, carrots and other young vegetables are covering more and more space by the day, exploiting any warm, moist spells. Within its heat-giving walls this garden is gearing up to supply Highgrove's kitchen with a choice supply of many Royal favourite ingredients.

Very few visitors to Highgrove use the Front Drive – even His Royal Highness almost always uses the Rear Drive. A pair of elegant but not over-imposing metal gates, set between ashlar stone pillars, and a small gatehouse guard the entrance from the main road. It is a surprisingly unassuming entrance, just a relatively small opening set in a stretch of Cotswold stone wall, closed off with gates which were a wedding present from the people of Tetbury in 1981. Sweeping in off the road, the driveway is slightly curving, with an avenue of limes and bordered hedge on one side. Before you quickly come out from the shade of the surrounding planting, you are treated to your first glimpse of the wonderful, expansive Parkland of Highgrove.

A visitor quickly realises that this property belongs to someone with definite style and ideas about gardening and the landscape. The areas of the Meadow are just starting to differentiate themselves from the mown verges beside the drive, and colourful drifts of crocus, winter aconites, primroses and daffodils are at this time of year either coming or going depending the time of the month, adding to the new Spring feel. The buff-coloured, fine-gravelled driveway snakes gently through the Meadow, with a thick

LEFT There are many cultivated and hybridised *Primula*, often scented. Here they brighten the Azalea Walk with swathes of blue *Scilla*.

BELOW The Front Drive, lined with lime trees, snakes through sheets of daffodils in the Spring. The rural feel of this entrance is enhanced by the grass strip in the gravel.

green stripe of grass that runs down its centre, which helps it to merge into the landscape rather than interrupt the wonderful rhythm of the age-old Parkland.

On both sides of the drive His Royal Highness has planted a row of lime trees about 10 metres or so apart so they afford the arriving visitor excellent views of the Meadow and then the house as you draw nearer. These are the weeping lime, *Tilia* 'Petiolaris', although this was not clear when the plants first arrived because the trees were dormant. It became apparent as the plants grew that only the two trees on the end nearest the house were in fact weeping limes – the rest were a different variety.

Once the error had been realised, the trees that were not *Tilia* 'Petiolaris' were replaced – hence the majority of the trees are a smaller size. As you approach the house in March, you sweep into the front entrance, past a group of rare cooking apple trees about to erupt into a show of pretty pink blossom. The beech hedge that lines the route on the right-hand side still has much of its russet Winter colour now, although this is just starting to be interrupted by Spring green buds breaking through. The gentlest breeze creates a quiet rustling among last year's desiccated leaves and the dense framework of twigs inside the hedge inevitably mean it is frequently busy with birds nesting, sheltering or feeding.

The height of the hedge is just below eye level, allowing tall people to look over to the Parkland beyond. The top is clipped to form an upturned 'A', breaking up the line beautifully. For those too small to see over it, the occasional Dorset gate offers views and access to the Parkland. Every detail of the entrance has been thought through carefully to create an approach that immediately tells you that you have arrived somewhere unique and exceptional. Looking up, if you see The Prince of Wales' Personal Standard flag flying, you know that the 'Head Gardener' is in residence.

The Rear and Front Drives connect at the chicken house, which has a seat built into the back so one can enjoy views of the Parkland and distant column.

# Rear (Main) Drive

Approaching Highgrove via the main, everyday entrance, visitors are instantly aware of the quality of style and detailing used throughout Highgrove. From the acorn finial, painted in the subtle 'Highgrove' shade of pale blue-green on the guard's gate to the tall stone building that shelters the policeman, it is clear that there is not a missed opportunity for detail on the entire estate.

Approaching Highgrove House from this more simple drive is every bit as enjoyable an experience as entering via the impressive front drive. This purposely narrow, single-track drive is delightfully simple and gently meandering, but from it you catch glimpses of key parts of the garden. On the right-hand side you pass the mixed woodland that contains the Stumpery and runs up to the old ha-ha, which defines the edge of the garden proper. Further on, you can see into the Meadow, which in March is bursting into flower thanks to the profusion of dark purple crocuses and yellow daffodils planted within it, cheerfully signalling that Spring is well on its way.

Having passed the entrance to the Orchard Room and main car park you are greeted by the Carriage Wash Pond. This was filled in when The Prince arrived, and the only clues that there had been something there were the few large trees around the slight indentation. The pond is a fascinating piece of history that would have been a well-used feature not that long ago, and so The Prince decided to excavate and restore it. In the nineteenth century horses and carriages were driven down the ramp into the fairly shallow water, to remove the worst of the mud and dirt from the roads. The water level is about a metre below the surrounding ground, which is retained by dry-stone walls and clad with native geraniums, ivy, ferns and other native colonisers. It is surrounded by hollies, hawthorns and other self-sown trees.

The Carriage Wash Pond is now a pool that is managed with basic maintenance and as such has a charming, romantic look and feel to it, which is enhanced by its historical context. The dead wood, which provides easy access to the water for mammals, and the richness of the 'natural' water make it a habitat that is rarely disturbed and abundant in wildlife. Expanses of water in natural settings are always quickly colonised, and aside from the newts, toads, frogs and other amphibious creatures, many birds, including tawny and little owls, kingfishers and chiffchaffs, have been seen here.

The Rear Drive links up with the Front Drive and between the two is the Gothic chicken house and pen. The fencing around the pen is constructed from beautiful cleft oak; tall verticals two metres high alternate with ones 150 millimetres lower to create a staggered top. This intriguing design confuses deer and foxes so they refrain from leaping over. The chicken house was a generous gift from The Prince of Wales to his ornamental fowls on his 50th birthday. He has quite a collection of hens as they are frequently given as presents. Richard Craven designed and built the structure, mostly in green oak, with hinges and door latches made by a local blacksmith. 'It also has

an aggressive four-foot-tall steel cockerel finial made by a sculptor friend, David Howorth. Cockerels always seem quite mad with power because they have all those females under their control and he interpreted that idea very cleverly'. Richard Craven usually asks clients, 'How do you want the building to make you feel when you see it for the first time?' The Prince's response was immediate, 'I want something that makes me say, "Oooh"', which indicated to Richard that he could go slightly into the realms of fantasy. You have the perfect view of the Parkland from here, with the column in the distance. Here you can find peace and quiet, with just the mesmerising antics and sounds from the contented fowl to entertain you. Anyone who keeps chickens will know that this must indeed be a sublimely restful place to escape the more pressing parts of life.

# Sundial Garden

The Sundial Garden is still essentially the same today as it was when first laid out in 1981–82. Plants such as the easy evergreen *Viburnum tinus* often still bear their mini, white, star-shaped flowers in March, which have been blooming throughout the dark, Winter days. The pale-blue evergreen *Iris unguicularis*, with its perfumed flowers from late Winter to early Spring, is perfectly sited here at the base of a warm wall. Other fragrant plants include the exquisitely perfumed, scrambling white jasmine, or poet's jasmine, and the stocky, robust, Mexican orange blossom, *Choisya ternata*.

The initial design included the addition of a paved terrace, conveniently sited in front of the house. Immediately beyond the terrace are the six bold and beautiful, geometrically shaped, box-edged beds. At this time of the year masses of daffodils and hellebores spill out of them; the daffodils providing a clever visual link to those lining the avenue that frames the grass path to the Kitchen Garden. Tucked up by the house you are treated to fat, dark magenta hyacinths 'Woodstock', whose delicate scent lingers on the air.

The terrace was built by Fred Ind, a veteran employee of Highgrove. In the spirit of the environmentally conscious ethos that permeates Highgrove, Fred lifted York flagstones from the back entrance, cleaned them up and relaid them as the terrace for the Sundial Garden. A circle of bricks a few metres out from the sundial were also laid within the grass. This piece of hard landscaping reinforces the importance of the sundial as a focal point in the space.

This intimate garden has a secluded atmosphere and the proportion of fabulously planted borders, lawn, hedging and climbers hugely exceeds the amount of hard surfaces. All this contributes to the soft, restful atmosphere of the space; it is somewhere that makes you want to sit, linger and enjoy, savouring the carefully selected colour palette of planting in the borders.

The six planting beds are edged with low box hedges and now have clipped yew shapes on the corners, which were designed by Prince Charles. They are strong and very extraordinary; the top is formed by flattened trapeziums, which have horizontal square top and rounded bases.

ABOVE All of the many beautiful gates designed by Willie Bertram have careful detailing and suit the architecture of the garden perfectly. This gate leads you onto the Lawn from the Sundial Garden.

RIGHT Early and colourful Spring plants in the Sundial Garden bloom amongst home-grown and home-made coppiced willow and hazel structures.

Their darker foliage stands out well against the brighter green of the box and they are symmetrically arranged around the central access, which runs out from the house down towards the Kitchen Garden.

It is one task setting out the Sundial Garden but quite another maintaining and developing the planting for future years. When Prince Charles started gardening at Highgrove, he was quite a novice, but he was extremely keen to learn. There was a lot of work involved, as the whole garden was continually being developed and continues to be so to this day, so ongoing maintenance is equally crucial.

It was concluded that in order to develop the horticultural side of the garden The Prince needed a Head Gardener who was also an experienced plantsman. David Magson, at just 27, came to Highgrove straight from Myerscough Hall, the Lancashire college of agriculture and horticulture. He quickly realised the work was not always predictable. 'One year,' remembers David, 'I had ordered a full quota of bulbs to plant, but suddenly it seemed everybody in the whole world decided to give Prince Charles bulbs as a present. We had a huge shed full of them and they took weeks and weeks to plant. When Prince Charles came back from his travels he could not see any sign of our planting and wondered what on earth we had been doing! He realised, however, the following Spring when there was a tremendous show!'

As the garden at Highgrove has taken shape over the years, many interested experts have come by to give advice and proffer suggestions. Among these were Pamela Schwerdt and Sibylle Kreutzberger (previously Head Gardeners at Sissinghurst), who showed the team their technique for making hazel domes around individual shrub roses, which Prince Charles was extremely taken with.

They collected green whips of hazel, just over a metre long, in March or a little earlier, and formed a series of

overlapping hoops in a circle around the edge of the rose. The rose branches were then pulled and bent over and tied to the hoops equally around the edge. In effect you end up with a domed rose, and because the branches are bent down, they produce many more blooms.

Today, many of the willow structures are made by the gardeners at Highgrove from home-grown and coppiced willow plants. Every Spring Helen Lomberg, an experienced willow weaver and sculptor, comes to Highgrove for a day or so and shows any new students or gardeners traditional techniques and methods with willow to reinforce the team's skills. They make beautiful circular columns used all over the garden as plant supports, including in the Sundial Garden. Here, they are planted up with sweet peas, to create towers of non-stop colour and to fill the green room with their heady fragrance.

# Meadow

Highgrove is famed, and rightly so, for its flower-studded Meadow. Its striking laidback informality contrasts sharply with the classical formality of the building and the surrounding ornate hedge. The large expanse (almost six acres) creates a refreshing breathing space to counter-balance the busier areas of the garden. The Meadow changes at an ever increasing pace from February until it is cut down from mid to late Summer. The bird and insect activity is equally busy in Spring, and this juxtaposes with such a visually restful area making it a fascinating place to linger.

During March, shadowy circles of purple crocus spring up around a fair number of the meadow trees. These circles are about three metres across and consist of thickly planted clumps of two types of crocus: the light purple 'Remembrance' and the darker purple 'Flower Record'. When used in this subtle way, crocuses are magical, appearing quite different to how they look when they are more frequently planted in a rather random and less considered fashion.

Daffodils highlight the walkways, mostly the bright yellow nodding heads of 'February Gold' and 'Jenny'. The area of the Meadow between the Lily Pool and the Lime Avenue sees a profusion of native daffodils, *Narcissus pseudonarcissus*, which bloom in March, explaining why this part of the estate is named on historic maps as the 'Daffodil Meadow'.

When Prince Charles started to create the gardens at Highgrove, his concerns about the dwindling numbers and disappearance of many wild flowers, such as the corn cockle and cornflower, were growing. There was an increasing awareness that old meadows and woodlands were being replaced by intensive arable crops. This sparked fear about the detrimental effect this was – and is – having on the balance of the natural environment.

So Prince Charles, determined in his quest to heal the countryside, asked Lady Salisbury for advice on suitable wild-seed mixtures for his Parkland to enable him to transform it into a meadow. He also wanted to find someone knowledgeable in this area who could advise

LEFT This reclaimed gate was found and adapted for Highgrove to frame the view from the more formal Sundial Garden across the wild Meadow.

RIGHT Sculptor Joe Smith's slate pots, made by using a technique similar to dry-stone walling, sit on the border of the Meadow and Winterbourne Garden in a sea of box planting.

him on how to develop the land into a rich and beautiful habitat. Lady Salisbury then introduced him to her friend Miriam Rothschild, the famous scientist and expert on fleas, worms, butterflies and wildflowers. Miriam subsequently exchanged many visits with Prince Charles, showing him her re-creation of natural habitats, her plantings and seed harvesting systems, and advising on seed mixtures and methodology while also recommending and supplying mixtures to use at Highgrove. Miriam had been told that it would take a thousand years to re-create a medieval hay meadow. She replied she would make a reasonable replica in fifteen.

The seed source initially used to recreate a traditional hay meadow in the old Parkland beside the house was a selected blend sourced from a Site of Special Scientific Interest (SSSI) in Northamptonshire. The selected species were carefully chosen so that they included some of the types that occurred locally to Highgrove, and that would bloom from early May to July. The mix consisted of a range of annuals and perennials, such as ox-eye daisies, cowslips, bird's foot trefoil, self heal, timothy, meadow-sweet and yellow rattle. This initial blend was referred to as 'the Gloucestershire Farmer's Nightmare mix' for the headache that these particular varieties gave farmers when growing on arable land.

The seed was drilled directly into the pasture but the initial results were disappointing for Prince Charles. The Parkland had been established for many years, and although it did not have hugely rich and fertile topsoil, the conditions would have favoured the already established grasses over the introduced wild flowers.

Slowly, after two or three years, Prince Charles noticed a few ox-eye daisies; then year by year the numbers of flowers appearing increased. In fertile soils, grasses usually outstrip wild flowers, but removing the cut grass from the area each year helps it to slowly reduce the fertility levels.

Prince Charles works with the Wiltshire Wildlife Trust to regularly carry out species counts within the Meadow. In 2008, one such count found a vast increase in the number of different plants establishing themselves. Even wild orchids are settling in well (The Prince counted over 400 in one afternoon and nearly 2000 were recorded in 2013) and, according to the current Head Gardener Debs Goodenough, 'Prince Charles knows exactly where all the clumps are, and each year he is thrilled to be discovering new ones.'

Southern marsh, common spotted, bee, and green winged orchids, which come and go, are so far found to be colonising the Meadow in various areas and after another 30 years of the same management systems, the diversity and numbers found should increase.

LEFT Many bulbs (here *Narcissus* 'Ice Follies') are planted in the Meadow but with restraint, predominantly using drifts of single cultivars.

ABOVE *Crocus* 'Purpureus Grandiflorus' and 'Remembrance', plus the odd white crocus grow in clumps in the Meadow. Any orange crocuses that pop up are rogued out.

The use of green hay to enhance the diversity of wild flowers in a meadow is a much-practised method. Clattinger Farm Meadows (owned and managed by the Wiltshire Wildlife Trust) has an arrangement with the Highgrove estate whereby they donate green hay, which has the advantage of containing a higher proportion of viable seeds than dry hay. Debs Goodenough, who has had a range of experience of developing and managing wild flower meadows, including those at Osborne House on the Isle of Wight, explains the importance of using this vital ingredient: 'You cut the hay just before it is ripe, usually from mid-July onwards, then it is baled immediately and brought over. We open up the bales straight away (to prevent it heating up) and then we just kick the hay around. It may look unusual but it works well.' The Meadow at Highgrove must be cut and ready to receive the hay before it is spread, to ensure maximum effectiveness.

Miriam Rothschild also advised Prince Charles on planting up the verges beside the drive; here annuals such as cornflowers, corn cockle, scentless mayweed, corn marigold and field poppy featured in the planting plan. This seed blend was another custom mix of the now-famous 'Farmer's Nightmare', but perennials were added to the verges too, at Prince Charles's request.

This mixture was hugely successful, adding a fantastic mass of impressionistic, eye-popping colour in the first years. The problem, however, in maintaining this balance is that poppies, moon daisies and other annual weeds of wasteland and arable crops require regular soil disturbance or cultivation in order for their populations to be sustained. This is difficult in a grass verge situation. For a few years the team got round this dilemma by cultivating narrow strips through it to encourage the reseeding of the colourful annuals. Now the perennials are so well established that there is no longer the need for the colour boost from the annuals, and Nature can be permitted to design its own planting scheme, with minimal intervention.

## Kitchen Garden

The Kitchen Garden is waking up quickly at this time of year; by the end of March it often looks very different to how it did at the beginning of the month. It has also changed significantly since The Prince sowed his very first crop of vegetables here. The roses on the arbours are now mature; the goblet-trained fruit trees have developed character and are becoming gnarled and beautifully knobbly, while many wall-trained fruit look like part of the architecture as they have melded with the rustic old walls.

On a sharp, bracing Spring morning you can see icy white coverings of frost dusting the vegetables. The two mature damson trees that sit in two of the triangular beds are covered with a haze of small, white flowers that hopefully will result in a heavy crop of fruit later in the year. Twenty full crates of violet-black damsons is not an uncommon harvest here at Highgrove, and they are traditionally made into a festive damson liqueur.

The fruit trees that have been immaculately trained on the walls look their best now, having been carefully and expertly pruned during the Winter (with the exception of the stone fruit trees, which are pruned in July). The wall-trained cherries and gages are looking promising already, with their lines of soft, welcome blossom stretching out over the brickwork. In the evenings in late March the flower buds on the naked pear trees begin to fatten delightfully, and many have already burst into a mass of snow-white flowers. These too snuggle up tightly against the mellow brick walls, which glow with warmth as they absorb the low, invigorating evening sunshine.

The construction of these walls is interesting; those that face south were built slightly higher than those opposite, presumably because shade is less of a problem here. The brickwork, which is pockmarked all over from generations of gardeners' nails and wire fixings, has recently been rewired so that in March, all the fruit trees and roses have been newly tied in and resemble works of art. The horizontal branches are attached to the wires using hessian ties a good five centimetres wide – a favourite method of Prince Charles as it is strong, looks natural and does not chafe the branch.

Trained pears are a huge royal favourite, which explains why there are so many varieties trained on both the south- and west-facing walls. Pear 'Beurre Superfin' is the choicest; this little-known variety is a delight to eat, having a crisp firm flesh that is juicy but not over-sweet. Surprisingly these pears have been known to support some unusual wildlife as they grow and ripen over the Spring and Summer months. One year, when these trees had become quite full and bushy, a pair of ducks that obviously liked the pond and the general ambience of the garden decided to build a nest in them. Other, rather less welcome visitors occasionally manage to steal themselves into this enclosed garden. One bold rabbit crept in when a gate was fortuitously (for the rabbit) left open – it was six months before the team of gardeners managed to catch up with it!

One of the most eye-catching parts of this garden are the mixed borders which flank the main central path that runs roughly north to south. The beds either side of the path mirror each other; in April they start to wake up and deep, generous swathes of daffodils, among which *Narcissus* 'Yellow Cheerfulness' and 'Old Pheasant's Eye', line the entire length of the back of both sides, providing strong, wide slices of bold Spring colour. 'Yellow Cheerfulness' is the most eager arrival, blooming earlier than the others and enthusiastically offering up to four fragrant golden yellow flowers per stem. This variety is followed by the fantastically bright 'Old Pheasant's Eye' (*N. poeticus* var. *recurvus*). The tiny red-rimmed yellow cups of this variety are framed by pure white windswept petals, but their beauty is not all they offer, for they release a sensational fragrance in this sheltered space which lingers in the Spring air.

One of the most time-consuming jobs for the gardeners is harvesting, and because Highgrove's Kitchen Garden is productive year-round, there is no respite for them, even in the Winter months. Each week a wheelbarrow will trundle through the gate of the garden, laden with produce and cut flowers which have been picked to send up to the house or to London for The Prince. In March this barrow might well contain Brussels sprouts, leeks, a variety of brassicas, handfuls of lovage, parsley, rosemary and thyme, and perhaps some daffodils. All the produce is washed and packed up so it arrives in the kitchen looking fresh and enticing.

The chefs, along with Ed Bollom, the gardener who is responsible for the Kitchen Garden, and His Royal Highness, of course, have a say in the decision as to

WITH APRIL COMES THE PROMISE OF warmer, longer days and a spring in the collective step. It is a month of hope and activity, as Nature leaps into action and fast-forwards to a season of colour and plenty. The Arboretum in April is stunning; the overhead shelter from the old larch trees coaxes the colour from myriad varieties of exciting maples that thrive under their high, protective canopies. The Cottage Garden celebrates the arrival of Spring proper with an explosion of colour, the foliage gently brushing your legs as you voyage through it, seductively inviting you to notice its harmonious scents and textures. Over in the Lower Orchard the bees are kept busy among the burgeoning apple trees and the chickens, spurred on by the ever-lengthening days, begin to lay vast numbers of eggs. Taking in the new, fresh Spring air from the Terrace Garden you can see and smell the azaleas in the raised bed nearby, almost glowing as the levels of bloom increase, and linger to take in the rapidly changing views across the landscape as it fills with life.

BELOW In April, the chickens begin to lay their eggs and enjoy helping to control potential pests on the fruit trees in the Lower Orchard.

RIGHT and OVERLEAF The long, thin shape of the Cottage Garden is disguised by burgeoning, colourful beds.

# APRIL

'Spring sees a resurrection in the garden. A green haze shows on the hedgerows and willows and suddenly the grass turns from a kind of washed-out khaki to a freshly mown emerald. Hovering on the air is the magical smell of balsam poplars, their sticky buds exuding an evocative scent to gladden the senses. I have planted these trees in strategic positions around the garden to reward the early visitor with an exotic aroma. Now is the time to welcome the flowering cherries and some of the early *Malus*, while forget-me-nots and tulips start to embroider the Sundial Garden. On the Terrace, the lady's mantle (*Alchemilla mollis*) springs back into life from what appear to be dead clumps and the *Philadelphus coronarius* 'Aureus' reappears in its golden finery.'

*Rhododendron*
'Loderi Sir Edmund'

what vegetables are to be grown. There are certain royal favourites that will be grown as a matter of course, such as the purple Brussels sprout 'Rubine', (quite demanding to grow) and the purple carrot 'Purple Haze'. These are not just grown for their novelty value, but also because they contain high quantities of the antioxidant anthocyanin, and The Prince believes they taste so much better.

In March, the gardeners start to make sowings of basil, broad beans, broccoli, cauliflower, sprouts, lettuce and peas, mainly in plugs in the greenhouse. Potatoes are also planted if the weather is promising, and will be fleeced up lovingly to hurry them along and protect them from early frosts. Prince Charles loves home-grown potatoes, so one whole bed will be devoted to them (moving annually in

rotation). 'Red Duke of York' is a firm favourite, with its purple-pink skin and moist yellow flesh. Another favourite is the 'Pink Fir Apple' – three whole rows will be devoted to this versatile and delicious spud which can be boiled, steamed, roasted or used in salads. It is a late maincrop variety with a peculiar knobbly pink skin, but its unattractive appearance hides a delicious, distinctly nutty taste and waxy texture.

LEFT Some daffodils were here when The Prince arrived at Highgrove and many have been given as gifts.

ABOVE The Kitchen Garden produces stunning colours throughout the year and now, tulips and daffodils sway among the vegetables and herbs.

# Cottage Garden

Huge changes take place in the Cottage Garden during the month of April, but every year our capricious climate means this month is unpredictable, each one bringing forth different conditions and challenges. Most years, however, this month sees tulips, foxgloves, cornflowers, forget-me-nots in blue, pale blue and pink, and honesty adding clear Spring colour among the sea of new foliage of the many Cottage Garden favourites that are blooming. Tucked in by the wall near the Indian Gate is a wide bed full of many golden plants, including the yellow acer *Acer platanoides* 'Princeton Gold', whose golden leaves turn a greeny yellow later in the year. The early-flowering rose, *Rosa xanthina* 'Canary Bird' is budding up, ready to flower shortly on its reddish-green arching stems clad with its ferny foliage. The soft, clear yellow, single blooms are produced in one exuberant flowering. The strong gold-yellow of choisya, golden variegated elaeagnus and loud forsythia is tempered by the lush foliage of the surrounding herbaceous plants.

The plan of the beds follows a meandering pattern and is interspersed with narrow grassy paths that encourage you to get right up to and almost in among the planting. A few key structural plants in strategic places add definition; repeated clumps of *Hebe rakaiensis* create domes in key places at the front of beds and contrast and support more ephemeral planting. There are beautiful, undulating mounds of hebe, with the younger, newer plants melding beautifully with the old and masking all their bare mature wood.

As you travel from the east end of the garden, nearest the house, you see the small Mediterranean Garden tucked in by the south-facing walls on your right. Just beyond this is a much-used sunny spot, which serves as Prince Charles's outdoor office when weather permits. It is located in front of a lowish, curving stone wall that divides the swimming pool from the Cottage Garden. However, in showery Summers the constant to-ing and fro-ing of cushions, chairs and paperwork had become an irritation, so in 2012 a green oak Summerhouse was commissioned to act as temporary cover when needed, and was finished in April the following year.

A little way beyond this is a unique circular bench with six individual seats carved into it. A yew column fills the centre and the legs of the seats are filled with sculpted box hedging. It was designed by the Bannermans and carved by the masons from Hereford Cathedral in 2006.

Carrying on up the garden, the linear space appears wider as it is punctuated with island beds and trees and the curves become more accentuated. A mulberry tree stands surrounded by grass, with a timber crutch supporting a lower limb. The tree is a cutting from one at Hampton Court Palace that was planted by Henry VIII, but despite its pedigree and beauty, it sadly fruits poorly.

Further up, having passed the holm oak (*Quercus ilex*), you enter the penultimate section of the Cottage Garden, where the snaking path continues but the linear borders flanking the path are dissected by long buttresses of stepped yew. Each of the eight border sections is variously colour-themed: blues and pink, a hot border, a cool border and various other combinations.

ABOVE *Tulipa* 'Mariette', a highly decorated Lily-flowered tulip, brightens the Cottage Garden.

Currently, Prince Charles is experimenting with combining pink and yellow, inspired by some Tibetan textiles. This will look most colourful from March to May, with camellias, lilacs, flowering currants, dicentras, primulas and forsythias all in bloom. True to Highgrove's experimental and evolving nature, Prince Charles has said, 'It might be very odd – but we'll see!'

In another section, blues and purples provide highlights in July with delphiniums, buddleia and larkspurs. These beds are rather like an artist's palette, with the royal artist and gardener playing and experimenting with different tones, colour balances and shades, matching and contrasting.

More drama stems from inanimate objects within the garden; a series of brilliant yellow-painted wooden benches is placed at the foot of the north-facing shaded yew hedge, which appears almost black by contrast. Before the benches were painted yellow, Prince Charles had initially found this area had become 'rather gloomy', but his solution to use the unusual but stunning yellow colour immediately transformed the space.

There are many more structural and design developments here over the years: a timber pergola was built to lead visitors from just beyond the northern end of the terrace to the stable yard, with a third entrance leading into this new Cottage Garden. A further couple of timber arches were placed along the length of the Cottage Garden, which served to split it into two. These timber structures have since been replaced by a fine stone pergola designed by Charles Morris.

This corner of Highgrove illustrates why being an artist and a gardener is such a winning combination: making the most of the stunning backdrop that is the house, affording the visitor seductive glimpses of both the building and the meadow over the lower curves of the hedge.

BELOW The Prince's decision to paint the benches yellow brings the north side of the yew hedge sharply into focus, creating a stunning backdrop.

RIGHT Cherry trees are a royal favourite and in April, they are smothered with white and pink cherry blossom.

# Meadow

The Highgrove Meadow is aglow in April. As the daffodils start to fade, the herbs and wild flowers get into their stride and the drifts of the ever-popular cowslip (*Primula veris*) provide charming pockets of colour. The height of these plants (which when thriving will reach up to 30 centimetres) makes the umbels of nodding, fragrant, bright yellow flowers stand out as they peer above the surrounding grasses. The foliage of the Meadow cranesbill, *Geranium pratense*, starts to go from strength to strength now, covering patches of grass and building up the strength the plants need to deliver a profusion of their pale-blue flowers in June. The bacon and egg plant, *Lotus corniculatus*, jostles to take its place, gearing up to present its yellow flowers in May. It is a familiar plant, also called bird's foot trefoil, and is so widespread that it has around 68 other common names too. Many other wild flowers are becoming more evident now, some well established while others are emerging as self-sown seedlings, having been sown directly in late Summer or indirectly from the bales of green hay that were scattered over the Meadow.

The tapestry of wild flowers and bulbs which make up this meadow is just one of the highlights of the six-acre site. The clever configuration of the other spaces that border the Meadow means that it appears framed when seen from many viewing points: either by the long lengths of embellished yew hedge, the woodland that forms the Stumpery, Arboretum or Winterbourne, or by the two avenues that stride through it. Trees have been planted through the space, supplementing the few huge trees that initially formed part of the wider Parkland around the house, including an impressive old oak and an ancient sweet chestnut which give the scene a sense of history. Newer plantings of trees, generally positioned at wide centres to facilitate mowing and to allow them to develop into a good shape, have been added over the last 30 years under Prince Charles's direction. These include the balsam poplar (*Populus balsamifera*), which is a great favourite of Prince Charles, due to the balsam odour that is released. Festooned with sticky buds this tree is an insect paradise, home to a range of caterpillars and moths. There is a fine, unusual collection of *Aesculus* (horse chestnuts) in the Meadow too, as well as other notable specimens such as the famous 'Boscobel Oak', *Quercus robur*. A plaque below it reads:

*These trees are direct descendants from the oak in which the son of Charles I, later Charles II, successfully hid from Cromwell's soldiers after the Battle of Worcester in 1651, and presented by the Forestry Commission and the Tree Council to commemorate their wedding in July 1981.*

In April the work of moles is evident, where they 'are tolerated but not encouraged'. They are not eliminated purely because, although the look of a meadow or lawn is not improved when littered with hills, these mounds do open up the areas of grass, thus creating space for wild flowers to germinate.

Gracing the Meadow near the Stumpery is a woven willow figure made by Emma Stothard, who visited Highgrove just after The Prince's much-loved Jack Russell, Tigga, had died. She collected materials from the willow bed and then sent a beautiful woven and lifelike form back as a thank you to The Prince for award of a loan from The Prince's Trust, which enabled her to start her career. Another spectacular gift sits alongside these willow weavings in the form of some toadstools carved from Highgrove's oak by a north Yorkshire farmer.

Encouraged by the huge success and interest that his Meadow generated, The Prince decided to try to encourage the development of more land in this way. As the country prepared to celebrate the sixtieth anniversary of Her Majesty Queen Elizabeth II's coronation in 2013, Prince Charles had decided that a fitting way to commemorate this historic year would be to establish 60 new 'Coronation Meadows', building on the success of the Jubilee Woods Project which was underway. The Prince masterminded the Coronation Meadows project, calling together many of the relevant organisations of which he is patron or president in order to obtain their advice and help. These included Plantlife International, Caring For God's Acre, Cornwall Heritage Trust, Garden Organic, The Foundation and Friends of the Royal Botanic Gardens, Kew, The Friends of Conservation, The National Trust, The Scottish Wildlife Trust, The Wildlife Trusts and many, many more. The project involved finding sixty existing species-rich meadows all over the country and using them to act as donor meadows to supply seed to parcels of land that could be set aside for the creation of new meadows.

It is a testament to The Prince's passion for the environment and persistence and drive for achieving his goals that these meadows were not only established but will be protected from development and carefully managed, providing a legacy which can be enjoyed by many future generations of man and wildlife.

Camassias, both the short *Camassia quamash* and the taller, pale blue *C. leichtlinii,* naturalise well, creating a sea of blue in the Meadow.

# Terrace Garden

The views from the Terrace Garden are spectacular and illustrate how the twin influences of painting and gardening affect Prince Charles's approach to the design of his garden. All the key views of the house at Highgrove, especially from significant areas such as this west terrace, are carefully framed, as if seeing an ever-enticing series of framed pictures. The views here are expansive, but are deliberately interrupted by objects and planting to delight the eye, not just in the foreground, but right through the middle distance and into the furthest corners of the garden.

Standing in the Terrace Garden, your eye is directed towards the Dovecote which sits over a third of a kilometre away from the French doors that lead out from the house.

It is in the foreground of this view that you see the partially enclosed Terrace Garden, with its range of scented plants chosen by Prince Charles, and four mature, beautifully gnarled olive trees underplanted with piles of low-growing Mediterranean plants.

Although these trees appear as if they have been there for years, they were in fact planted in 2010, as a much-appreciated gift from a friend and neighbour. April is a special month for these trees, as this is when their Winter fleece jackets are removed and their characteristic silver-grey foliage is revealed again, still looking quite full despite the time of year. In the middle of the four olives is a small ornamental pool, which reflects light into the garden and mirrors the elegant foliage of these dramatic trees.

A series of four stone steps takes you down from the French doors onto this informal and friendly garden. It feels protected despite its expansive, dramatic views, helped by the presence of low stone walls built at a comfortable height for sitting.

His Royal Highness decided to create a backdrop to the wall by planting low box hedges behind it, as if to form the back of a bench. The informal, billowing, generous planting that sits immediately within the walls provides a comforting sheltered feeling, making the Terrace Garden feel like an extension of the house and very much a beautiful outdoor garden room.

Several signature plants that feature throughout the garden, such as large, lush clumps of *Choisya ternata* and golden philadelphus, are planted in this Terrace Garden. There are also several of His Royal Highness's favourite ceanothus, *Ceanothus* 'Puget Blue', repeated at intervals. Commonly known as the Californian lilac, this looks stunning at the end of April, smothered in dense clusters of tiny, dark blue flowers. When these are over, the small, neat, dark green foliage is an excellent backdrop for the more colourful plants that perform around it.

At the centre of the terrace, there is a shallow octagonal pool, its top flush with the paving, and its base covered with pebbles that are visible through the crystal-clear water. A few glistening pebbles balance on top of an old millstone, and a small jet of water gently bubbles up from its centre, washing over the millstone so it sparkles in the sun. It makes an ideal water bath and drinking bowl for the many birds that live here, which can regularly be seen on the pebbles, having a long drink or a perky preen.

Just a few metres along the house wall is a raised bed which has been cultivated for acid-loving plants. His Royal Highness has had a passion for these plants for many, many years, probably stemming from when he used to spend enjoyable days with his grandmother, the Queen Mother, at Royal Lodge in Windsor, which had its own impressive display of rhododendrons.

Prince Charles was given a fabulous collection of rhododendrons and azaleas by the late Edmund de Rothschild, as a wedding present in 1981. Eddy de Rothschild was famous for restoring Exbury Gardens

in Hampshire and also for breeding several new rhododendron hybrids and developing the Solent Range of Exbury deciduous azaleas. Initially this magnificent gift had been planted in the woodland area, but the plants did not thrive there, so a new home had to be found for them. The solution was to build a raised bed conveniently located near the house.

Many gardeners encounter problems when they grow acid-loving plants in artificial situations such as this, but for a long time, this bed – which is visible from many windows of the house – looks spectacular, especially in early Spring.

LEFT Stunning pots of *Rhododendron* 'Alfred', a richly flowering plant with a compact habit, surround the central pool of the Terrace Garden.

ABOVE *Tulipa* 'Spring Green' with *T.* 'Van der Neer', an extremely old but sturdy and substantial variety, are in pots on the Terrace Garden in Spring.

Among the dramatic plants are many sweet-scented azaleas, which fill the air with their fabulous fragrance in Spring, and the hybrid dwarf *Rhododendron* 'Blue Tit', which reaches just 60 centimetres high and bears clusters of blue flowers in April and May. Another rhododendron, *R.* 'Yellow Hammer', which is larger, reaching to just over a metre, grows here too. As its name suggests, come May, it is smothered with rich yellow flowers, but then it earns its place all over again in Autumn when it blooms once more and puts on a further show of dramatic colour.

Unfortunately, the bed began to lose some of its acidity and as Highgrove is organic, the gardeners are limited in what they can apply to the soil to increase its acidity. As a solution, a seaweed tonic with iron is applied fortnightly during the growing season and in addition, the Head Gardener, Debs Goodenough, applies new acid soil transferred from the Arboretum, lots of leaf mould, and mulches the bed heavily with shredded bracken to help increase the acidity. Once the soil had been prepared and invigorated, more rhododendrons were added to raise the bed, including varieties lifted from Birkhall in Scotland and also new additions such as *R.* 'Königstein' and *R.* 'Rosinetta'. Debs is also planning to experiment with planting varieties of rhododendrons that have been grafted onto the recently developed Inkarho rootstock, as these rhododendrons are more tolerant of less sheltered conditions, exposure and limey soil.

Through all this work and dedication, this bed, which contains some of The Prince's favourite plants, was turned around in the Spring of 2013 and restored to its former glory.

BELOW The Terrace Garden is separated from the Lawn by low box hedges; the pepperpot buildings and oak pavilion dominate the outskirts.

RIGHT Early in the year, crocus flowers fill the gaps in the paving; later, lady's mantle appears, followed by lily of the valley and other treasures.

# Lower Orchard

This two-acre paddock is fascinating, full of a wide range of fruit trees of varying ages and types. By the end of April many of the trees are covered in beautiful shades of blossoms. Here, as in every other part of Highgrove's great gardens, working with Nature is a key consideration, so in one corner there is a large, timber, traditional bee house given to His Royal Highness on a visit to Slovenia. A plaque inside the house reads:

*'Republic Slovenia, Home of the Carnolian Bee. 1998.
Anton Pavel Edeśan CZS'*
(CZS stands for Čebelarska zversa Slovenije' –
the Slovenian Bee-keepers Association)

The bee house is alive with the activity of the inhabitants of the ten hives within. As soon as the sun shines, the bees are out, working the orchard flowers as well as the comfrey, foxgloves and other early blooms that occupy the surrounding gardens and fields. The chickens, which nest in one of two houses nearby, (each catering for one hundred birds), are busy scratching, bug-hunting and enjoying the longer days, sunshine and new, fertile grass. The sound of the mower in the distance, somewhere in the chicken-free area (their position is rotated to keep the grass lush and fresh), is comforting, partly because of the evocative smell of the freshly mown grass, but also because it reassures you that Spring is well and truly here.

On two sides of the orchard the boundary is formed by a Celtic hedge, planted in 1995, which was created by the famous sculptor David Nash.

The brief was to create a hedge that would act as an environmental barrier to the elements and would also double as a work of contemporary art. Nash planted the young plants (violet willow, ash and sycamore) along with supporting stakes, some sloping one way, some the opposite so that they crossed over each other. Over the subsequent years Nash trained the whips so they weaved in and out of each other, hence the name 'Celtic hedge'. The idea was that it should look like a natural structure at first sight and then as you got closer, you would realise that there was more to it. Nash would occasionally return to Highgrove, over an eight-year period, and weave the structure to achieve the look he wanted. Initially there

were problems – the horses, who are always voracious nibblers, became rather partial to the tasty young shoots. Apologetic letters arrived from The Prince for lack of fencing, but once this was in place, the structure began to take shape. Prince Charles, accompanied by his faithful Jack Russell Tigga, enjoyed strolling round to the hedge to admire its progress.

The hedge is now maintained by the gardening team, who cut back the older wood, arch down the young shoots and secure them in place to create the appearance of a series of overlapping arches.

In 1982 only half of the area that is now the Orchard was planted. In the same year, Vernon Russell-Smith drew up a scheme which shows four blocks of apple and pear

LEFT One hundred chickens were introduced to the Lower Orchard in 2003 and since then, their numbers have doubled. The eggs that they produce are sold in the locality.

BELOW The Slovenian Bee House allows the beekeeper to tend to the ten hives within it under shelter, rather than being outside in all weathers.

trees flanked on two sides by five crab apple trees (*Malus hupehensis*), which are excellent pollinators. The plan included several different varieties of apple, including 'Discovery', 'Sunset', 'Ellison's Orange' and 'Blenheim Orange', and 'Beurré Hardy' pears. The small crab apples are harvested and used to make crab apple jelly for the Highgrove Shop.

In 1999, the Cheshire Landscape Trust gave His Royal Highness a gift of many fruit trees, which had been raised or associated with the county of Cheshire. Just after this, in 2000, Will Sibley, a grafter and fruit expert, was called in to do some pruning and grafting of the fruit trees in the Kitchen Garden and he also got involved with advising on the new planting that was needed to fill the whole area.

These new trees were planted, as the others had been, in a grid of rows about 5 metres apart in both directions.

More recent plantings have introduced a rich and varied selection of fruits to the existing group of trees. Nick Dunn, a fruit grower and expert in this field, came and surveyed the collection in 2011 to clarify the names of some of the trees that had been forgotten. There are many unusual quince trees, including *Cydonia* 'Leskovac', 'Ekmek' (a Turkish variety) and 'Agvambari', as well as traditional old fruits such as medlars, mirabelles, many different pears, damsons, gages, plums and apples.

The Orchard continues to develop and thrive, as more trees and varieties are added to the already impressive collection.

# Arboretum

In the Arboretum at this time of year, some beautiful collections of the very best specimen acers are beginning to proudly unfurl their delicate leaves, above a vibrant and vivid understorey of naturalised bulbs and herbaceous plants. The amount of sunlight that penetrates through the Arboretum's canopy is relatively high now, as the huge larch and other established older trees do not come into full leaf until later in the season. The bulbs make full use of these welcome pools of sunlight and respond by carpeting the woodland floor with vast expanses of colour.

*Narcissus* 'Thalia' is one of the many exhibitionists in the limelight now. Planted in massive swathes, it lines the emerald-green grassy ride from the Kitchen Garden up to the Odessa statue. This daffodil is a star, with its multi-heads of trumpets (three to four per stem) that are greeny-white in bud before they open to reveal a

charming pure white flower. As with all daffodils, their strappy foliage must be left to die off for a good six weeks before it is removed to allow the bulbs to continue to grow – otherwise the chances of a stunning performance the next Spring are jeopardised.

Other bulbs that are colonising and stealing the limelight now are celandines, *Chionodoxa luciliae*, and *Scilla siberica* 'Spring Beauty'. The latter is an excellent naturaliser and it has a more delicate head of the characteristic sapphire bells than many of the more clumpy flowers of other scillas. Later, *Narcissus* 'Hawera', another multi-headed daffodil with creamy yellow flowers, will follow on from the *N.* 'Thalia' to provide a continuous carpet of colour for a few more weeks.

If you can pull your eyes away from the action on the woodland floor, you will notice many exciting new developments at eye-level too. The smaller trees, mainly cherries and Japanese maples, are awakening with a spectacular show of blossom and richly vivid foliage.

Some of the Japanese maples (this term usually refers to maple tree cultivars from *Acer palmatum*, and may include those from *A. japonicum* and *A. shirasawanum*) are repeated in several places, as they are firm favourites of the royal gardener. *Acer palmatum* 'Shindeshojo', the Spring ruby tree, is one such statement tree. The new leaves that start to emerge in March and April are bright ruby red, turning to pale pink later in the season. It has a wide-growing, yet upright habit with light twiggy branches, giving it an airy, delicate feel.

One acer that has not fully leaved up at this time of year but still stands out is *Acer palmatum* 'Sango-kaku', which has extraordinarily luminous orange-gold new and old wood, although the youngest twigs emerge as a coral pink. These delicate young trees are positioned next to a group of *Rhodendron sinogrande*. This is one of the

LEFT *Magnolia* 'Athene' has huge flowers up to 25cm across, with ivory-white petals that become rosy-purple at the base.

RIGHT *Acer palmatum* 'Shindeshojo' has beautiful ruby-coloured leaves and is a maple grown for Spring rather than Autumn colour.

mammoth-leaved evergreen rhododendrons with huge architectural value; the leaves can be up to a metre long and are a shiny dark green with a glistening silvery fawn indumentum (a fur-like surface) on the undersides.

The inclusion of magnolias in many parts of the garden highlights another royal favourite. The Arboretum offers fairly good conditions for magnolias – dappled shade and fertile, moist soil. Here they are mainly planted as single specimens rather than in groups. The frost-hardy flowers of *Magnolia* 'Eskimo' in particular stand out. Its delicate white flowers are deceiving; despite their fragile appearance they will withstand any late hard frosts, but when the petals do fall, they dust the woodland floor like a carpet of snow. *Magnolia* 'Susan' is stunning when in bloom; in April its purply-red flowers are vibrant and their

sweet smell drifts through the warm Spring air. Camellias – reds, pinks and white – thrive here, some having been recently moved from Llwynywermod, The Prince's residence on the Duchy Estate in Wales.

Apart from acers and cherries there are also several crab apples planted here, including *Malus sylvestris*, the common crab apple, which grows wild in many parts of Britain. It is the parent of the orchard apple and several ornamental crab apples and bears white or pale pink blossom, followed by small fruits.

It would be all too easy to lose days in the Arboretum throughout the year, examining the different species of trees and marvelling at their colours, and April is certainly no exception.

*Ceanothus*
'Puget Blue'

# MAY

'This is the month that I relish the most, when everything is new and fresh. The glistening lime greens, yellows and oranges of oaks and beeches fade so fast that every moment has to be savoured. The fleeting pink of unfurling copper beeches has a magic of its own, as does the short-lived blue and yellow partnership between the camassias and massed buttercups in the Meadow. The apple trees are in blossom, the bees are once again in the garden and it is a time to give thanks for the miracle of creation in all its glory.'

T HE WARMTH OF THE SUNSHINE IN MAY encourages rich growth throughout the garden, and every corner at Highgrove now looks sublime. The colour levels in the Sundial Garden, especially from the camassias, which draw your eye through to the masses planted in the Meadow beyond are spectacular, the Stumpery takes on a lush and mysterious feel as all the new foliage of the ferns and hostas unfurl, lapping up the dappled sunlight that breaks through the creeping canopy above. The established apples in the mini-Orchard by the Orchard Room now create a bold pattern of green and blue with the catmint (Nepeta × faassenii) in flower, circling around the trunks. However, the brightest star in the Highgrove firmament in May has to be the Meadow.

BELOW Views to the Arcadian Parkland over some traditional cleft oak fencing with a five barred gate.

## Meadow

Highgrove's greatest jewel in Spring is vibrant and humming now, full of blooming wild flowers which are being visited by a plethora of insects and birds. The scene changes dramatically in different lights and is constantly busy, open all hours of the day and night. As twilight beckons, the Meadow is equally arresting: bats replace the birds, and moths and owls are on the hunt for insects, pollen or small mammals.

As the days get longer and warmer the bulbs in the Meadow become more dominant. The showy cammasias, both the shorter, deep violet blue of *Camassia quamash,* which sometimes start to flower at the end of April, and *C. leichtlinii*, which is usually a paler-blue and taller than the former, are firm favourites.

GATEFOLD The purple and white wisteria on the south wall are now flowering together, blending the two colours.

PREVIOUS This avenue, which leads from the Sundial Garden to the Kitchen Garden, was originally planted with the crab apple *Malus* 'John Downie', before being replaced by fastigiated hornbeams.

BELOW and RIGHT *Camassia leichtlinii* 'Caerulea' with *Allium hollandicum* 'Purple Sensation' grows in the Meadow. The bulbs are planted in large quantities by lifting a turf flap with a spade and putting in several bulbs per 'pocket'.

These beautiful plants are deceptively easy to grow, tolerating a range of soil conditions and happy in either sun or semi-shade. In grass they naturalise well as long as they are left uncut until the leaves have faded, which usually happens in June. *Camassia quamash* is ideal for naturalising in grass as it is vigorous and reaches just 35 centimetres high (shorter than most varieties). A little later on, and carrying on throughout June, the more unusual white cammassias come spectacularly into flower. Many tulips were originally planted in the long grass and they would have now been preparing to perform. Beautiful colour coordinated swathes of 'Burgundy Lace', 'Negrita',

OVERLEAF The oldest trees in the Meadow and Parkland were most likely wood pasture trees dating from around 1665.

'Negrita', 'Attila' and 'Purple Prince' – all in varying tones of deep red and purple, with staggered flowering times – lined the hornbeam avenue. Unfortunately many of these varieties succumbed to Tulip Fire, a fungal disease that can fatally affect bulbs, especially if their leaves are damaged by bad weather. The only solution to the problem was to have a tulip-free period, to try to eradicate the disease, and so instead thousands of *Fritillaria meleagris* were planted here. The snake's head fritillary, or chess flower, as it is also commonly known because of the intricately chequered pattern on its bell-shaped flower, is a curious and beautiful plant which stands quite tall, between 12 and 30 centimetres high, and bears deep purple or white flowers. It is quite rare in the wild, and these bulbs

were a much appreciated present from the British music legend and environmentalist Sting.

Whistling Jack, or *Gladiolus communis* subsp. *byzantinus,* is a corm that produces blooms of a rich magenta colour, flecked with white. The stems emerge from the ground in April, but it is in June that it shows itself in its full glory. Reaching a height of around 60 centimetres, it lifts its flowers high and adds an unashamedly loud touch of brilliance to the Meadow. This plant will often self-seed, so it is sustainable, but if new Autumn bulb and corm plantings are required they must be protected over the Winter months, otherwise they are prone to damage from pheasants, squirrels and other wildlife that frequent the Meadow.

# Dovecote

This fine, traditionally styled building stands at the end of the Lime Avenue and aligns with the west-facing French doors that lead from the house into the Terrace Garden, to create a strong vista. The Dovecote was the very first commission that David Blissett worked on as a qualified architect. He admits that pulling off this first commission for such a high-profile client was a fascinating and highly enjoyable experience.

David initially drew up three versions of the Dovecote, followed by models made from English walnut – a simple version, a Tuscan version and a Gothic version. He then gave these to Mollie Salisbury to deliver to The Prince. Things went quiet for a while until he was approached

by the estate builders, who informed him that a slightly adapted version of his Gothic model was being created.

The Dovecote was a gift from the Sultan of Oman and is dedicated to Sir John Higgs, who was secretary to the Duchy for many years. It was intended to have been built on a slight mound, to increase its prominence, and was designed to house doves. The materials used in its construction are traditional, fitting in beautifully with the local vernacular. Cotswold stone tiles were used for the typical steeply sloping tiled roof, with diminishing courses of tiles progressing upwards, the central circular building was created from coursed random rubble stone walling, and softwood (fir) columns support an overhanging roof at one end of the building, which provides a place to sit under cover and admire the views. As you approach the house from the driveway, the view of this building set against a woodland backdrop and highlighted by the Lime Avenue cannot fail to turn your head.

LEFT Fastigiated hornbeams were chosen for this avenue down the Meadow, which leads from the Sundial Garden to the Kitchen Garden, as their upright forms will not create too much shade for the Meadow flowers.

ABOVE The canopy of these lime trees is regularly raised to conserve the view of the Dovecote from the Terrace Garden.

# The House

His Royal Highness believes he visited just one house when he was searching for his new home. Highgrove was not an ostentatious, huge, grand property, but The Prince 'was rather taken by it, mainly because it had the remnants of a small park and some wonderful trees'. On first impression it looked stark, with next to no garden as such, but The Prince recalls how the quality of light that flooded in through the hall windows impressed him.

Highgrove was a property that definitely had room for improvement, both inside and out, and that in itself had strong appeal. The house was built in the 1790s in neoclassical style, but by the time His Royal Highness arrived in 1980, it had seen many alterations.

As you approached the house from the drive, the historic Parkland that surrounded much of the building consisted of huge old oak trees that informally punctuated the grassy acres. There were some more exotic specimens, too, including a Lucombe Oak (*Quercus × hispanica* 'Lucombeana'), a copper beech (*Fagus sylvatica* Atropurpurea Group), a walnut (*Juglans regia*) and a Spanish oak (*Quercus falcata*).

The eighteenth-century walled garden (albeit rather rundown and overgrown, with a missing section of wall) and a huge, ancient cedar of Lebanon which dominated the west-facing elevation were other elements that persuaded His Royal Highness that this was where he would like to take root.

The views of the house now as you arrive from the Main (rear) Drive are very different to those The Prince saw when he first arrived. Your eye is immediately drawn towards the house, framed and embellished by lines of pleached hornbeam trees and magnificent sculpted hedges to highlight the facade. This strong, architectural planting now anchors the house to its garden, while the informality of the vibrant Meadow planting connects the surrounding landscape.

It is not only the changes to the garden that have caused this transformation. Prince Charles realised that the solid parapet wall that ran around the top of the house 'did not look right'. It was too harsh and severe and contributed to the rather stark, neglected look of the property. He had

seen some houses improved with the help of Felix Kelly (a graphic artist, designer and well-known painter), so The Prince asked him for his opinion. In line with Kelly's ideas, the solid parapet wall was removed, and the small stone globes that had topped it were relocated by His Royal Highness to the Kitchen Garden. The solid wall was replaced with a visually lighter stone balustrade, embellished with some classical stone urns, matching pilasters and a pediment with a round window was added to the front elevation. By adding these details the rather heavy, foreboding look of the house was replaced with a feeling of character, elegance and warmth.

As you come up to the front of the house from the rarely used Front Drive, you see bold planting hugging the house, billowing up just above the base of the low Georgian windows. The Victorian porch (which was added after a fire in 1893), has a well-trained *Vitis coignetiae* on one side of it. This deciduous vine, which has leaves the size of generous dinner plates, turns scarlet-crimson in the Autumn, although it produces its best colouring on poor soils. It is pruned back vigorously every year to ensure optimum display. Either side of the crimson glory vine, as it is often referred to, are two golden-variegated ivies, *Hedera colchica* 'Paddy's Pride', which have central sulphur-yellow markings through the dark evergreen leaves. Tucked among is a jasmine, *Jasminum officinale*, which produces the familiar, highly scented, between mid-Summer and early Autumn, white flowers, whose delightful fragrance fills the porch and wafts into the hall.

The climbers are abundant all round the house, adding personality and helping the structure blend into the garden. The climbers are now happily established, so much so that they need to be reined in regularly to curb their natural ebullience, so in January a cherry picker is brought in to restrict the growth of the climbers to the top of the first-floor windows.

The planting around the base of the house is designed to have a strong presence whatever the time of the year, so a number of different evergreen plants have been included too, many of which are of a more intimate scale. A huge, beautifully shaped specimen of *Viburnum davidii*, with its

neat, deep green, corrugated leaves, erupts in June with flattened heads of tubular white flowers that will later develop into metallic-looking turquoise blueberries. Other plants that greet you by the front door are golden philadelphus with their light, romantic, almost honeyed scent, euphorbias, sweet-smelling roses and forget-me-nots, which tumble delightfully over the immaculately raked gravel.

As you look at the house, on your right-hand side is a tall, fine, tapestry hedge of holly, box, yew and other plants, clipped informally to form cloud shapes. This hedge starts at the edge of the Georgian facade, defining it and masking the transition between this and the newer part of the building.

If you stand with your back to the front door, the oval gravel drive in front of you is broken up by a large terracotta urn in the centre, which is surrounded by a small, oval lawn. At this time of year the pot is full of tall, pink and dark purple tulips; later there may be a mass of dahlias and in Winter a fine topiary yew may be placed there.

Looking over the urn, your eye is drawn to an exquisite view of Tetbury Church, which lies just over a mile from the door. This church, St Mary Magdalen, is purported to have the fourth highest spire in England. This view had to be kept clear (by covenant) until 1991. The owner in 1891

was William Yatman, a barrister, who sadly lost a son, and in his memory he paid for the rehanging of the church bells and some alterations to the church tower, which in turn guaranteed that the view would be kept clear for a hundred years. This idyllic view over the Parkland is still clear, and is framed by two mature, clipped holm oaks (*Quercus ilex*).

In May, as you look at the house from the Sundial Garden, you are entranced by the mass of wisteria that covers the lower two-thirds of the building. Only the purple wisteria was here when His Royal Highness arrived. He then planted the white wisteria over 25 years ago, and this has now covered the other side of the south elevation of the house. The two colours melded together to create a sensational, dramatic effect, with the pale, honey coloured walls of the house as the perfect backdrop.

The impact of the wisteria flowers is massive, and the blue colour range carries on in the borders throughout the Sundial Garden, with camassias, forget-me-nots, and purple lupins, and continues on through the gates into the Meadow where the camassias create a virtual sea of blue.

ABOVE Purple wisteria thrives on the south wall, looking sensational against the honey coloured walls.

RIGHT *Ceanothus* 'Puget Blue' produces beautiful blue flowers at this time of year.

# Terrace Garden

In May, the colour in the Terrace Garden is spectacular – tones of mauves, pinks and blues contrast with the brilliant greens. Four intense purple azaleas sit in terracotta pots by the pool, other pots are brimming with purple and pink tulips, and elsewhere, smoky mauve alliums tone with the deep purple sage leaves around the olives. Lighter blue forget-me-nots, mid-blue rosemary flowers and powdery blue spires of camassias that have sprung in from the meadow form a random, lively patchwork of colour that is the perfect foil to the fine stonework of the surrounding buildings.

In the evening light, the setting sun casts a warm red and flattering light over this secluded area, highlighting the rich purple tones. It is the perfect spot to relax after a stressful day and observe the wildlife, enjoy the plants and listen to the small, trickling pool.

The handsome 200-year-old cedar of Lebanon that stood just a few metres from the house was one of the reasons that Highgrove appealed so much to Prince Charles. The 18-metre tree dominated the garden and imparted a friendly atmosphere to the house, with its huge, dark emerald green plates of foliage, while its spreading limbs provided dappled shade to those sitting on the terrace. The arching frame of this magnificent tree anchored the newer vista of pleached trees beautifully.

The tree did initially cause concern, not least because cedars possess an alarming habit of suddenly dropping whole limbs and branches that may easily weigh two to three tons, even on perfectly calm days. In 1998, some surgery took place, removing the unsafe limbs, and a replacement cedar was planted 15 metres away.

In 2007 the original old cedar was looking in bad shape. There were bracket fungi (*Ganoderma*) colonising it which caused decay to the heartwood, which in turn was making the tree even more prone to unpredictable limb dropping or blowing over. Finally, with huge regret and a heavy heart, the decision was taken to fell it. It was too large for complete removal so His Royal Highness decided to raise a building over the butt of the cedar to celebrate its life. Prince Charles put this original approach to one of his favourite craftsman, Mark Hoare, who specialises in structures with an ecological slant. Mark kept one of the lower branches and at special request, left a hole in the roof for a self-sown oak sapling to grow through and provide a living ceiling to the structure so it will become truly integrated with the landscape.

Conceptually Mark used the Tetbury Church spire as inspiration, which seems fitting as the cedar is a very spiritual tree, featuring in many Christian psalms. From the house you can now see two spires: Tetbury Church and the cedar building, and they complement each other very well. The finished building is somewhere between a square and a circle, with a curving timber oak frame. The roof, made of oak tiles, finishes in a square with the spire or obelisk that is cut from Highgrove green oak. The building sits in a sea of bold-leaved hostas which are arranged around its base, their new foliage looking especially crisp and fresh in the Summer sun.

When the building was initially completed it caused quite a stir. The new, quite bright, blond colour of the oak was highly noticeable in what had been the most restful, understated space in the garden. Now, as the oak is weathering to its characteristic silver-grey and the oak saplings grow more each year, the distinction between the trees and building is beginning to blur to become one. It was a challenging project, and in twenty years when the oaks really come into play, it will most likely be regarded with the same admiration and affection that the original cedar tree enjoyed.

LEFT The pepperpot buildings were designed so Prince Charles does not feel exposed with his back to the Lawn.

OVERLEAF The oak pavilion is an epitaph to a felled cedar. Young sapling oaks grow at the base and soon the trees and building structure will merge.

# Sundial Garden

The Sundial Garden is a stunning sight in May, with its deep borders producing firework-like displays of colour, just ahead of the delphinium extravaganza that will shortly follow in June. There is a sea of charming forget-me-nots (*Myosotis sylvatica*) and not just in the quintessential, beautiful clear blue colour we are most familiar with, but also in the white and pink forms too. They are left to self-seed to ensure more flowers for following years, but if necessary the seedlings are thinned to around 150 millimetres apart to encourage them to grow into strong, leafy plants. Camassias are also at their peak now too, and the deep blue flower spikes of *C. leichtlinii* subsp. *suksdorfii* Caerulea Group, at 60 centimetres high stand well above the carpet of forget-me-nots. They are arranged in the beds so that they line the central grass pathway and help guide your eye out to the Meadow, where they link up with more camassias planted en masse.

The colour and content of the Meadow at this time of year stops most visitors in their tracks. Mixing up the dominant blue theme in the beds are a range of alliums, their bobbles of strong magenta, purples and clarets standing up proud above the low hedge. The superb deep mauves contrast with not just the blues but also the neat green lines of the fresh new foliage of the box hedges.

There used to be a timber archway leading out of the Sundial Garden into the Kitchen Garden. The archway needed to be replaced, so Isabel Bannerman found some beautiful but dilapidated cast-iron gates in a reclamation yard in Bath and managed to get them repaired and restyled by Bob Hobbs, a blacksmith from Upper Langford.

He added some exquisite touches, such as The Prince of Wales gilded feathers, which were wrought by Alan Cooper. The fine metalwork, complete with scrolls, feathers, crown, foliage and finials, has the highlights

picked out in gold leaf and this gilding never fails to catch the sunlight. Gold leaf, rather than gold paint, is a more economical way of gilding metal because it does not fade as paint would do.

These gates are an extremely clever addition, and one that immediately transformed the views in and out of the garden, opening its doors to welcome visitors to explore the more formal Sundial Garden and the relaxed Meadow beyond. They elevated the space, adding stature and marrying the garden beautifully to the house.

The gates are set off perfectly by the huge, ball-topped, black-green yew piers that frame them, and help to emphasise the transition between the gardens. On the Meadow side, two huge terracotta pots, which were a gift, stand sentry. They come from the Aegean side of Turkey, where they were used for storing olive oil, but now, complete with simple metal stands, they are planted with big specimens of a *Hydrangea macrophylla* variety.

Looking through the handsome gates into the Sundial Garden you can see repeated specimens of the beautiful multi-stem forms of *Magnolia stellata* 'Royal Star'. They are arranged centrally in each of the six beds and their leafless stems in April/early May are covered with their delicate, spidery white blossoms, which echo the white of the snowdrops which were flowering here earlier. These blossoms also catch the eye on the other side of the hedge and peer through the 'framed windows' in the yew.

LEFT The Sundial Garden begins its burst of Summer colours in May. The dark green of the yew contrasts with the more lime green of the box hedging.

BELOW In the corners of this garden, immaculately trained groundcover roses, *Rosa* 'Grouse', are planted and pulled down over the urns. Prince Charles enjoys working in the garden and new views are afforded with each time of day, season and year.

# Stumpery

In May the Stumpery is transformed as it fills with leaves and flowers which burst forth, softening the angular architectural lines and clothing the earth in a rich tapestry of greens.

The understorey of the Stumpery changes rapidly as the masses of ferns unfurl their fronds and the clumps of hostas throw out their leaves on a seemingly daily basis. Light levels are still relatively high now as many of the trees' canopies have not fully opened, so the foliage sparkles in the dappled pools of sunlight that filters through the trees and brings the sylvan carpet to life.

The lilac *Syringa komarowii* opens its mauve-pink, sweet-smelling flowers, which hang in panicles rather limply, making the clusters appear to be nodding. It is a rare but beautiful shrub. Another shrub with similar but brighter red-mauve hues is *Weigela florida* 'Wine and Roses'. The foliage is olive green with a wine flush that darkens as the months progress.

The Stumpery temples, arches and mounds were built in the Summer of 1996 over a period of about six or eight weeks. The two main temples are made, unusually, from chunks of green oak (as opposed to stone) which were cut to size at a local sawmill. The 'columns' are made from huge, impressive vertical slabs of oak over 30 centimetres wide and 15 centimetres deep. All the green oak was wire brushed and sanded by hand to create a smooth finish.

Sourcing unusual pieces and artefacts was indeed a labour of love. The tympanums, the triangular faces of the pediments, which are often enriched with relief sculpture, are meticulously decorated with white roots that the Bannermans found washed up on the shores of a Scottish loch. These add to the woody, organic feel of the temples. The insides of the temples are decorated with many layers of a honey-coloured wash and on the back of each one is a beautifully carved quote. One, from Horace, translates as: *'they think virtue is just a word and a sacred grove just sticks'.* The other one says, *'Find tongues in trees, books in running brooks, sermons in stone and good in everything.'*

You enter the heart of the Stumpery through an archway constructed from beautifully gnarled old stumps, stacked together ingeniously. Building the arch from the

BELOW The two green oak temples in this clearing are a part of the original Stumpery, and are decorated with roots that were washed up on the shore of a Scottish loch.

RIGHT The durable timber of the Sweet Chestnut stumps provides sheltered crevices for ferns, primroses and sweet woodruff.

stumps was an organic process. 'They are rather like jacks, the metal ones you play with as a child – they bind together,' the Bannermans explained, although they have used metal pins and rods to control them in certain positions, such as over the arches. Sourcing the stumps was a stroke of luck. At Cowdray Park, West Sussex, the stumps from a wood of sweet chestnuts, which had been cut down for use during the Second World War, were re-discovered during the great storm of 1987. Lord Cowdray saved the stumps for Prince Charles; they had been growing in sand for years, meaning the tree stumps had rotted to their core, leaving just the resilient and spiky parts behind.

It was a memorable moment for the policeman on the gate when they arrived piled high on a huge lorry. The garden guides saw them arrive too, and looked intrigued. Prince Charles simply said teasingly, 'Just you wait!'

Excitement throughout Highgrove continued while they were working away on the sharp structures. The Princes, then 14 and 12, would bomb around the woodland in a hair-raising fashion on their bicycles watching it all happen, and the Bannermans prayed they wouldn't cut a corner just that bit too tight …

While the structures were being completed, various guests came to see the new creation. The then Duchess of Devonshire, Deborah Cavendish, was enthralled by it. Another guest was so amazed she was moved to tears. Prince Philip remarked with a sparkle in his eye, 'When are you going to set fire to this lot?'

The planting in the Stumpery has developed greatly over the years since its inception. Originally, the scheme was intended to include mainly hostas, but then as the strong character of stumps and buildings unfolded it was decided to plant huge drifts of ferns too, which have a rather primeval feel to them that enhances the 'other-worldly' atmosphere of this garden. As the Stumpery has expanded in size so has the planting palette, and now there is much more colour, especially in shades of creams and greens.

# Orchard

The south exit of the Orchard Room extends onto a charming, small Orchard. In May the apples are smothered in blossom and the blue catmint (*Nepeta* × *faassenii*) encircling the base of the old apple trunks is in full flower too. This is how you imagine the perfect orchard to be – well-trained, goblet-shaped apple trees that look happily entrenched and laid out in perfect rows. The dry-stone walls that partially surround the space are slightly swooped down in the middle on the side next to the drive, allowing you to see into this perfect mini-orchard on your journey past.

Despite its idyllic air, the orchard is important for its significant collection of fruit trees. They were presented to The Prince by the Brogdale Horticultural Trust in 1991 and include some of the oldest and rarest apple trees in the country. Many have interesting names such as 'Ten Commandments', 'White Junety' (ripens first and last), and 'Rivers Nonsuch'. When the government sold Brogdale in 1991, many people were concerned that their important research and vital collection of 2,300 apple trees would be lost. Prince Charles was greatly concerned too, not least because he feared that the genetic material would be lost forever. As a result, the Duchy of Cornwall helped to provide the funding for the newly formed Brogdale Horticultural Trust to purchase the trees and the land.

Apart from the apples that are sold in the shop in Tetbury, lavender oil was also produced from plants grown at Highgrove at the base of the trees in the orchard, for a time. Lavender is the most popular essential oil; it is also a firm royal favourite and is used in the Highgrove range. It is a herb that is renowned for its abilities to soothe, to revive and to ease aches and pains. A free-flowering form called 'Imperial Gem' was selected to produce this oil, and each year the gardeners would pick four or five large black bags full of lavender flowers and add to the bags various thymes and other herbs. Unfortunately the lavender plants did not perform well because they did not get enough sun, so in 2013, they were replaced with the more tolerant herb – catmint.

In the centre of the Orchard is a piece of intricately carved stonework mounted on a few courses of random rubble walling, designed by Geoffrey Preston, a ceiling decorator who is renowned for his stucco and plasterwork. While studying stone carving, Geoffrey visited a famous mosque in Süleymaniye, in Istanbul, and photographed the columns heavily decorated with the traditional '*muquarnas*', from which he gained his inspiration. Geoffrey contacted Keith Critchlow, who is President of the Temenos Academy and the Founding Director of The Prince's School of Traditional Arts, to see if he could find something similar to the carvings

The Orchard outside of the Orchard Room includes some of the oldest and rarest apples in the country. In May, the apple trees are smothered in blossom, with blue catmint (*Nepeta* × *faassenii*) encircling the base.

in Istanbul. Professor Critchlow offered Geoffrey a similar stone carving that had been made by an artist who had studied and trained at The Prince's School. Photographs of the carvings were sent to The Prince, who said he would be delighted to include one in his garden. This column capital is now displayed upside down on four stone supports in the Orchard.

The entrance to the Carpet Garden is from this Orchard and the doorway leading to it is framed by two quince trees, *Cydonia oblonga*, which, most unusually, have been fan-trained against the wall. Quinces are remarkably beautiful trees, and in May their translucent, large white and pale pink flowers are spangled freely among the foliage. In late Autumn, huge pear-shaped fruit hang against the wall, changing slowly from green to gold.

To complete the picture, climbing roses (growing on the reverse side of the wall in the Carpet Garden) have been immaculately trained down the wall to greet the quince. The occurrence of the mass of white rose blossom above the quinces on either side makes maximum use of this wonderful piece of Cotswold stone walling.

On the west wall, there is a fine *Magnolia grandiflora*, given to The Prince on the Golden Jubilee in 2002 by Pierce Brosnan. Further along this wall is a huge, old, rectangular stone trough with a fascinating metal circular disc on which is etched a complicated labyrinth pattern which came from the Healing Garden at Chelsea Flower Show in 2002 (designed by Ginny Blom). This wall was rebuilt some 20 years ago and is now part of the new cattle barn. It was rebuilt using recycled stone, brick and chalk from a reclaimed old barn that had been taken down.

Southern marsh orchid *Dactylorhiza praetermissa*
Common spotted orchid *Dactylorhiza fuchsii*
Bee orchid *Ophrys apifera*
Green winged orchid *Anacamptis morio*

# JUNE

'By now most of the colour is fading from the Arboretum as the salmon-pink *Acer palmatum* 'Shindeshojo' loses its lustre and the rhododendrons and azaleas sink back, exhausted after their brief spell in the limelight. In the Winterbourne Garden, the tree ferns are slowly unfurling their 'bishop's crozier' fronds, while the first roses burst into bloom – if the buds haven't already rotted in incessant rain. The growth in all the borders is exponential during this month and the longed-for delphiniums (one of my most favourite plants in the garden, if you can get them to grow properly) are almost ready to come out. To get the best out of delphiniums they need to be in massed ranks or in noticeable platoons, each one with a cane to ensure it is ramrod straight and at attention. The trees are all out in full leaf now and the orchids in the Meadow are revealing their pink and purple spikes. Having started with nothing 33 years ago, it is hard to describe the joy it gives me each year to see the ever-increasing number of orchids now appearing. In June there are two species in the Meadow – the southern marsh and the common spotted – with the occasional bee orchid from time to time.'

SUMMER AT HIGHGROVE IS ENCHANTING: the warm- coloured buff stone of the house forms a fabulous backdrop to show off the purple and white wisterias in the Sundial Garden, and the roses which smother the rose pergola release an intoxicating fragrance as you walk through towards the Cottage Garden. The planting in the Cottage Garden still has the strong exuberance characteristic of Spring and early Summer growth, which serves to increase the informality of these eclectic gardens. The Azalea Walk always has strong architectural appeal, but in June the highly fragrant azaleas entice you to stop and smell as you pass. Next door in the Kitchen Garden the planting has reached a crescendo, as the bright and bold colours of the central flower borders vie for attention with the cornucopia of tempting, tasty-looking vegetables and mouth-watering plump fruits. It is a month of plenty, wherever you look.

BELOW The colourful cushions of thyme are at their most aromatic in June and are covered with bees on a sunny day.

RIGHT The fresh Summer growth of the yew turns the wonderful shapes along the Thyme Walk golden again.

## Thyme Walk

Highgrove is famed for its magical Thyme Walk. There are few thyme lawns and walks left today, but they were very common in earlier gardens.

Apart from its rarity, the Highgrove Thyme Walk is even more exceptional because of its dramatic scale and the broad range of different varieties of thymes used. The fine, fragrant pathway runs west from the Terrace Garden towards the Dovecote for about 95 metres, and is composed of a mass of pillowy thymes, from the highly prostrate varieties to some that are more buxom and bushy. Although slightly scented all the year round, the cushions of pinks, purples, yellows, limes and greens are at their most aromatic from May to July, when they are in flower.

In Summer the carpet comes alive with bees who, as soon as the sun comes out, home in on these blooms and busy themselves working all the tiny blossoms to gather their vital nectar. It is a satisfying pursuit to take the time to look for tiny thyme plants where the pollination has resulted in new seedlings.

Before His Royal Highness started creating the walk, there was just a simple gravel path edged with fairly mature golden yew 'blobs' which lead out to a rectangular pond. Prince Charles had inherited the golden yew and was rather averse to the gravel, so the walkway was not to last long. Since 1984, oddments of leftover granite setts and various stone slabs from various projects had been saved and collected, so in 1990, His Royal Highness decided to oust the gravel and create a new hard surface from an interesting collage of the excess and salvaged materials.

In order to achieve a subtle weave of thymes and stone, everything had to be fitted carefully together so that it did not look contrived, then the joints were filled with soil so that the thyme would colonise the gaps and make the path a living fusion of soft and hard materials.

With an area as large as this to plant and tend, it is crucial to provide optimum conditions. Thyme can be short-lived (often lasting just a year or two) in wet soil, but in free-draining soil and sunny positions, plants can live for quite a few years, though it is often recommended that they are replaced every four to seven years.

His Royal Highness contacted Kevin and Susie White, who grew a National Collection of thymes at Chesters Walled Garden in Northumberland. They advised The Prince on the best thymes to grow and it was agreed that they would limit the range to about 20 of the most suitable varieties. One of these was *Thymus serpyllum,* which is a striking evergreen and aromatic native thyme that flowers profusely. Gardeners David Magson and James Aldridge took thousands of cuttings of thyme from Hexham Herbs (the Whites' nursery) and grew them on the current plants at Highgrove to bulk them up to provide the vast quantity needed to fill the path. These rooted within a few weeks, were hardened off then potted up. The Prince planted

all of them at weekends over a period of around three
months in 1991, between March and June.

Thymes establish very quickly and many of the
creeping ones soon colonise quite large spaces, so it was
not long before the massed effect of this organic and
colourful path created a beautifully interwoven tapestry
of scent, colour and texture that was appreciated by all.
At night, this important walkway was once used as an
entrance for guests. The guests were dropped off on the
drive at the top and walked down the pretty patchwork
path, which was lit by mini-night lights. It is not difficult
to imagine the magical atmosphere that is created through
the combination of the delicate scent of the thyme that
is released as it is crushed underfoot along a pathway lit
by moonlight and candles.

The golden yews that framed this walkway when His
Royal Highness bought Highgrove were slightly frowned
upon. They had been there for a good while and looked
mature, but their golden hue, resulting from the new
growth which is produced in late May or June, was
thought to be rather too brash and bright. Prince Charles
decided the yews could well be made into an asset, as their
maturity meant that they could be shaped into unique
pieces, so the path would be flanked with strong and
fairly instant punctuation marks. So The Prince asked
Highgrove's gardeners to clip them into eccentric shapes.
They relished the opportunity, although were slightly
apprehensive at the task they faced. Their work looks
outstanding now – beautifully bold with a wide range
of curious and clever shapes adding great weight and
interest to this significant vista.

Adding yet more weight and a similarly sculptured
effect to this strong sight line are the pleached trees,
which frame the outer edge of the garden. These 'frames'
are made from double lines of hornbeam trees that now
look sturdy and mature, structural yet elegant. In warmer
countries the original purpose of pleaching trees was to
provide welcome blocks of shade. Here though they are
used more as 'green architecture.'

# Sundial Garden

June begins the delphinium season and as this is one of Prince Charles's favourite plants, the garden is bursting with them. He loves to see huge, deep banks of delphiniums arranged with their colourful spikes, co-ordinated to dazzle with a sea of blues, purples and deep pinks. 'Every time I go to Chelsea I gaze in wonderment at them,' Prince Charles admits.

The Sundial Garden is an ideal home for delphiniums, as the soil, having been improved hugely over the years with the addition of lashings of home-grown compost, is moisture-retentive but free-draining. It is also deep and rich, and so can provide sustenance for these hungry plants. The thick hedge is an excellent filter for the wind and the perfect, dark, formal backdrop to highlight the colours and majestic forms of the delphiniums and lupins.

Many seasoned delphinium growers will emphasise this plant's huge energy requirement, and the importance of the soil's composition to meet this need all through the long growing season. Under the direction of John Ridgley,

Highgrove's Deputy Head Gardener, the garden team guarantees this by adding compost regularly. In addition, to achieve really good, strong spikes, an established group will have its number of shoots reduced to around seven or so to ensure that fewer, stronger spikes will be produced. Newly planted delphiniums may be reduced to around two shoots.

Staking is key to support the massively tall flower spikes. This is done by using one cane per plant, which is tied discreetly down the back of it when the plant comes into bud. When the flowers are over, they are dead-headed and cut down to just below the flower portion of the stem, maintaining as much leaf as possible, and a second, far less dramatic flush will appear later in the Summer if the growing conditions are suitable.

BELOW The Sundial Garden is now a heady, informal blend of purples, blues, white and pinks.

The dramatic show of vibrant colours from the delphiniums has been carefully orchestrated by Prince Charles. He is extremely particular about the shades of blues, purples and pinks that he grows here. His favourite varieties are *Delphinium elatum* 'Clifford Lass' (deep pink with a brown eye) and 'Amadeus' (a richer purple-blue with a large brown eye or bee), which are grown in big clumps in the beds nearest the house. The soft powdery blue of *D.* 'Loch Leven' with its white bee is planted with the more purple-blue of 'Cassius' in the two middle beds and 'Cymbeline' (a deep pink with huge florets) is mixed with 'Faust', an intense, gutsy ultramarine, in the farthest borders. These are all the majestic Elatum types which grow to around 1.6 metres high; they are generally easier to grow than the Pacific Hybrid types, which are shorter-lived and can be picky. Along the back of the borders, standing out against the yew hedge in June, are the reddish-purple flowers of the King Arthur Group, whose wonderful array of colours are variously highlighted at the beginning of the day by the low angle of the early morning light on one side, and by the warm evening sun as it dips down in the sky on the other.

Within these deep, lush borders a mixture of roses, herbaceous plants, tender perennials and bulbs provide spectacular colour before, after and alongside the delphiniums. Two beautiful roses are trained around woven willow crowns, which are planted towards the front of the first of the two large box-edged beds. *Rosa* 'Louise Odier' is an old Bourbon rose that continually flowers well, producing pale, almost lilac-pink blooms with a rich fragrance. These two qualities earn its place here, alongside the fact that it is widely thought to be one of the most reliable and healthy of the recurrent-flowering old roses.

BELOW *Onorpodium acanthium*, the Scotch thistle, towers behind the vibrant delphiniums and white lupins.

PREVIOUS *Magnolia stellata* 'Royal Star' are planted in each bed in the Sundial Garden, and can be glimpsed through the yew windows surrounding the border.

RIGHT Varieties of *Delphinium elatum* glow in evening sinlight.

The other rose planted here is *Rosa* 'Winchester Cathedral', an excellent white, perpetual-flowering shrub rose, which arose as a sport of *R.* 'Mary Rose'. Its flowers are scented rosettes of typical Old Rose character, which are studded liberally through a good, dense, bushy, well-leafed and -shaped shrub, and as such it fits in well with its perennial neighbours. Also pepping up the colour levels are clumps of rich, purple-plum spikes from the *Gladiolus* 'Plum Tart'. This plant flowers from July to September and is superb for cutting and bringing indoors. However, it is tender so it has to be lifted and stored in frost-free conditions each Autumn.

Reinforcing the blue notes is another robust, tender perennial, *Salvia* 'Indigo Spires'. These plants are wind- and rain-tolerant, performing well whatever the climate chooses to throw at them. The salvias are repeated in the borders, giving cohesion to the beds and complementing the whites and magentas of the phlox.

The phlox varieties include the excellent white form, *Phlox paniculata* 'Alba Grandiflora', with its strong, quite willowy growth and pure white, fragrant flowers. Being drought-resistant, it performs well in dry Summers too. *Phlox paniculata* 'Border Gem', a fabulous old English variety, which has rich, deep purple flowers on stout stems, and starts to flower at the end of June, was also chosen to complement the neighbouring delphiniums.

Annuals enhance the colour levels further in a carefully coordinated scheme, with clumps of pink *Lavatera* 'Loveliness', various shades of sweet peas scrambling up willow teepees, pink cosmos and pink and white *Nicotiana* 'Whisper Mix'. Adding an extra boost to the pink and purple spectrum are a selection of dahlias, including the electric pink of *Dahlia* 'Fascination', which leads the cast, with the sumptuous magenta purple tones of *D.* 'Thomas A. Edison' providing a strong supporting role. *D.* Happy Single Wink and *D.* 'Bishop of Canterbury' are both great performers, adding purples and pinks into the mix later in the Summer.

The Sundial Garden is one that has seen much change and no doubt will continue to do so over the years. Delphiniums were not the initial stars here – before they took centre stage, pastel borders took pride of place for a good 16 years from 1982 until 1998, with only minor variations. One year, for instance, the Queen's racing colours of purple, gold, scarlet and black were used as the theme for a Spring display.

Following this, it was agreed to plant a garden of strong contrasts and so the Sundial Garden was bursting with 'black' and white flowers, which was quite different from the existing gentle pastels.

There are no really true black-flowering plants, but dark purple makes a good substitute. *Heuchera* 'Obsidian', with its dark purple-black leaves and tall red stems, was one of the favourite herbaceous plants, providing a long season of colour with its almost evergreen leaves. *Pittosporum tenuifolium* 'Tom Thumb', the dwarf evergreen shrub with reddish-brown foliage, was another. *Tulipa* 'White Triumphator' and dark purple *T.* 'Queen of Night' looked dramatic in Spring, together with variegated white honesty and foxgloves. As the season progressed, annuals such as the stately *Nicotiana sylvestris* 'Only the Lonely' and white cosmos joined the fray. The popular *Dahlia* 'Bishop of Llandaff', with its dark purple foliage, would be planted out now and any early orange flowers would quickly be removed – the colour scheme of this newly planted garden was strictly adhered to.

Apart from the strong and dynamic planting that has evolved in the Sundial Garden, four gifted busts of Prince Charles also needed to be positioned, and it was decided that these would be displayed within the niches in the yew hedge. Prince Charles laughingly thought that maybe the garden should be renamed the 'Ego Garden', but they have been discreetly set into the hedges, and are beautifully displayed, adding structural interest to the garden. Many visitors enjoy them, and they only add to the more personal nature of this garden.

# Cottage Garden

Although the Mediterranean Garden is a relatively recent development within the Cottage Garden, it brings with it an air of maturity. Originally it was known as the Box Garden, a space designed by Prince Charles in the centre of which was positioned a colossal terracotta pot lying on its side, with the space around it a mass of organic, loosely cut, cloud-pruned shapes that resembled undulating, green, well-puffed pillows. There were subtle contrasts in colour and texture within these shapes, as many different forms and varieties of *Buxus* were used. However, as box blight took hold across the gardens it was decided to replace these plants with many grey leaved species that would thrive in the relatively hot, sun-baked area.

Although a small garden, it has several clever touches. The boundary that borders the farm buildings has a high yew hedge with a flat top. The sides of this hedge are punctuated with carved alcoves with interestingly shaped terracotta urns set inside. The height of the hedge allows outward views to a group of stone farm buildings beyond, and these beautiful barns with their sloping sheets of Cotswold-stone roof tiles remind you that farming was

BELOW A toddler Prince Harry was once found hiding in this urn in the Mediterranean Garden.

the vital ingredient that led to the gentrification of the Cotswolds from the Middle Ages onwards.

On another side of the garden, the curving stone rustic and moss-clad wall that backs onto the swimming pool area rises gracefully as it twists round gently. A bust of Leon Krier (the Master Planner of The Prince's Poundbury development in Dorset) sits on a tall, modern, sawn-stone plinth immediately in front. The third side allows framed views between several of the circular dry-stone columns of the pergola, which lead you to the house or the stables.

The aromatic inside of the garden is composed of a mass of grey-leaved perfumed plants, with just a narrow winding path through them, which enables you to brush by and come in physical contact with these sensational silver plants. The garden is full of soft colour now, mainly blues and mauves. Many cistus are grown here, including *Cistus creticus*, a small shrub with shaggily hairy stems and purple rose-like flowers. The blue flowers of Jacob's ladder (*Polemonium caeruleum*), rosemary and the intense purple from *Erysimum* 'Bowles's Mauve' jostle alongside the lavender, of which there are several types, including *Lavandula angustifolia* 'Hidcote' and *L. a.* 'Imperial Gem'. The soft blue mauves combine beautifully with the various pastel-coloured sun roses, or cistus. The aroma of lavender is extremely soothing and this, combined

with the calming colours and hues and the simple layout make the Cottage Garden a cohesive and restful place.

As you enter the Cottage Garden via the Indian Gate, you see a climbing rose, *Rosa* 'Jude the Obscure', with its freely produced, pale-peach chalice-shaped flowers and strong fruity fragrance rambling upwards over it.

There are other striking plants here; in the corner of one of the alcoves of yew hedging, a large shrub, the bladdernut (*Staphylea*), produces a massive profusion of white blossom, and alongside it are large angelica plants with their massive umbels of pale green flowers, huge blowsy peonies in pinks and reds, lemon-yellow aquilegia and sumptuous dark purple irises.

BELOW A path of foxgloves leads to a stone obelisk marked York, Weymouth and Bath, a sixtieth birthday present from these Stonemasonry Colleges.

RIGHT The luscious Oriental poppy, *Papaver orientale* 'Patty's Plum', adds to the soft colour palette of this garden. It may produce a second flush if cut down after flowering.

A central drift of the resilient *Salvia nemorosa* 'Lubecca', together with nepeta, geraniums and delphiniums, sweep through the Mediterranean Garden, which is now considered part of the Cottage Garden.

Plants and pots are often given to the royal gardener. It is not easy to find appropriate gifts for a Prince, but most benefactors are wise to the fact that he is passionate about his garden. Pots arrive at Highgrove on a regular basis, and instead of dotting them around the gardens, a cluster of them are collected together in an informal area of longer grass and bulbs near the Indian Gate. Here, a group of nine or ten Italian, African, Jordanian and South African pots of various heights are artfully arranged and planted, allowing them to show off some seasonal specials.

There are other artefacts arranged here too: several busts of people who have influenced HRH Prince Charles, Highgrove, or other important and influential individuals. A bust of Maurice Macmillan (son of Harold), Viscount Macmillan of Ovenden, who was an MP and lived at Highgrove, was made by Angela Conner in 2010. It sits in an alcove in the fine yew hedge, now surveying a very different scene from that which he left. Another is a bust of Sir Laurens van der Post (by Frances Baruch), a close friend who had a significant influence on the royal gardener's life. Another friend who has a home here is Dr Alan McGlashan, the psychiatrist and intrepid First World War pilot.

When Highgrove was bought by the Duchy of Cornwall, there were overgrown laurel bushes at the extreme western end of the Cottage Garden. Prince Charles contacted Julian and Isabel Bannerman to have a look at them, thinking there may be a way of making a walkway or tunnel. Now as a result, as you leave the Cottage Garden, you walk over a perfect path of stone cobbles. This first starts as a right-angled path, which changes direction by way of a large circle of radiating stone. At the centre point of the circle is a stone obelisk, which sits on a tripod and is marked with 'York, Weymouth and Bath' – the significance being that it was given to Prince Charles for his 60th birthday by these three stone-masonry colleges. This path now leads under the laurels that have been lifted and trained to form a dark, atmospheric tunnel, which serves to enhance the approaching contrasting view of the dramatic, wide-open and often bejewelled Meadow.

# Rose Pergola

As you head towards the house at the end of the Cottage Garden, you pass under a sumptuously wide pergola festooned with roses and wisteria. Although this garden is a walkway connecting the Cottage Garden with the Lawn and Terrace Garden, the scent, colour and lavishness of the beautiful roses trained in spirals up the posts stops you in your tracks. The mass of blooms from favourite climbers such as *Rosa* 'Sir Paul Smith', *R.* 'Blush Noisette' and *R.* 'Madame Alfred Carrière', with their pinks and whites and the abundance of lilac blue, contrasts effectively with the surrounding honey-coloured stonework.

The garden itself has a reassuring, enclosed feel to it, with low Cotswold stone buildings connecting with the house and forming a boundary along two sides of the garden. Although Highgrove is a large garden, many of the spaces within it are surprisingly intimate and friendly, which is one of the reasons many visitors find it such an enjoyable garden to visit.

A large yew at one end near the raised acid bed that abuts this area helps shelter the garden. The wall of the building that encloses the long west-facing side of this space also protects it, and is planted with wide groups of shrubs that thrive here. The lime-green flowers of *Euphorbia amygdaloides* var. *robbiae* jostle next to herbaceous anemones and the glossy leaves of *Choisya*, furnishing the outer edges of this corridor.

This pergola, designed by Charles Morris, replaces a timber version that was originally built primarily to define this walkway from the west terrace to the stable yard at the far end. It was agreed that many of the beautifully established climbers that are enjoyed today and were happily clambering up the old structure, should be conserved.

The circular columns, which look as though they are built of dry-stone walling, were built fractionally to one side of the old structure to prevent too much root disturbance to the climbers when the foundations were being built. The pergola was a 50th birthday gift to The Prince and the Highgrove staff used over seven tons of green oak in its construction.

The narrow pathway under the structure is patterned by shadows from the large oak beams that span the pillars. The paving is an informal jigsaw of York stone paving, bricks and stone setts with a mosaic of surprising finds peppered within, including fascinating stones commemorating the Silver Jubilee and the Diamond Jubilee and a small cast-metal disc with 'ER 1970'.

Upon exiting the oak pavilion and looking back, the focal point of the view is a fine, wooden, Chinese Chippendale-style bench painted in a striking livery of pale blue and strong pink, which also incorporates The Prince of Wales' feathers in its design. Prince Charles is highly experimental with colour and the bright, original combination used here lifts the whole feel of the space.

'I was really taken by Yves St Laurent's garden in Marrakesh, the colours and combinations on pots and seats for example, and thought I must try that,' Prince Charles revealed, 'So I got a huge swatch of eighteenth-century colours and had great fun experimenting and thinking what colour would go with what.'

Imposing yew buttresses frame this stunning resting place and in June, a magnificent wisteria of lilac flowers covers the Cotswold stone building it backs on to. There is an old lime tree to one side of the end of the pergola that leads you towards the Cottage Garden. This has a mass of bushy young lime shoots around its base, known as epicormic growth, which is common to certain lime species of this age. Ever conscious of allowing Nature to take its course where possible, His Royal Highness decided to treat this fuzzy growth without removing it and instead had it shaped into a piece of quirky lime topiary.

At the end of the vista from the Cottage Garden down the short spur of the pergola that leads to the house is a special three-way teak seat designed by Stephen Florence. This was completed in 2003 and is known as the Laocoön Bench. Stephen Florence worked with architect Leon Krier for many years and so designed this bench as a homage to him, incorporating Leon's designs from previous work. Two green glazed oil jars are set on either side, which were a birthday present to The Prince from the Duchess of Cornwall. A fine stone plaque is fixed to the wall behind it, which depicts Laocoön and his two sons in a copy of the original that is kept in the Vatican Museum, in Rome.

Perhaps the most amazing elements of this small garden are the large and extraordinary shapes that are growing in the grass on either side of the Pergola. These represent the five Platonic elements of Earth, Water, Air, Fire and Ether, which are on one side, and the first five of the thirteen Archimedian solids, which are on the other. They are grown on slightly raised mounds, which gives them more prominence.

The views facing west and framed by the pergola are stunning. Initially at the Terrace end, you can see over a lower 'scallop' in the grand yew hedge. In the centre of this scallop a superb lifelike topiary eagle with wings spread is precariously perched on a yew ball. Looking under the wings you catch an enticing glimpse of the Lawn and the pleached hornbeams beyond. Further along at the other end you can look into the Mediterranean Garden, which is now bursting with colour.

# Azalea Walk

His Royal Highness spends a lot of time working abroad, seeing fine gardens, architecture and landscapes along the way. The Azalea Walk was inspired by a visit to Villa Gamberaia in the hills of Tuscany, where Prince Charles was impressed by the huge, regularly spaced urns set on mown lawns to show off fine specimens of azaleas. He explains, 'I saw this wonderful walk and I remember being so struck by these enormous terracotta pots with huge azaleas going all the way down and thinking, how amazing!'

You can enter the Azalea Walk from one of four entrances, but whichever route you choose, there is an air of serenity. This linear garden has a charmingly simple rhythmical composition; a line of terracotta pots flank both sides of the gravel path, planted with stunning pairs of azaleas that are flowering in late May and June.

In 2010 it was decided to renew the soil in the pots using acid soil brought in from Sandringham, and six highly scented azalea varieties were selected for their yellow, gold and pink tones. The varieties chosen included *Rhododendron* 'Silver Slipper', which bears large white and pink flowers, *R.* 'Nancy Waterer', which has golden yellow flowers, and *R. luteum* 'Purple Leaf' and *R.* 'Princess Margaret of Windsor' for their yellow flowers in various shades.

The planting in this enchanting garden is always cohesive and often bold. Although the azaleas are the star in May, the ferns, which have replaced the mown grass around the pots in years gone by, add to the sombre, relaxing feel of the space. Climbing roses, *Actinidia kolomikta* with its green leaves splashed with pink and white, and clematis add colour which responds well to the low angled light from either side that is thrown on this much-used walkway.

As you walk down the Walk towards a statue of Diana, the Huntress, the high wall that borders the Kitchen Garden is clad with lush greenery, adding to the serenity of this evocative garden. The climbing hydrangea, *Hydrangea petiolaris*, proudly displays its showy white flower heads, spotlit by shafts of evening sun that dodge between the tall yews.

The opening from the centre of the walk to the Arboretum was added in 2004 to link this increasingly important collection of trees and shrubs with the core spaces of the garden. This more recent entrance into the Arboretum has a carved stone transom which was created by Anna Ricketts and the Egyptian hieroglyphics read:

*The garden is a reflection of the stars in the sky*

'Similarly, the garden is a reflection of the gardener and develops around a series of ideas and decisions that he or she makes,' adds Prince Charles.

Many influences have affected this gardener in his numerous walks of life, and some striking busts have been created and placed here, known as the 'Wall of Worthies'. These include two by Angela Conner, of Sir John Tavener, the composer and musician, and Deborah Cavendish, the Dowager Duchess of Devonshire; two by Aidan Hart, of Patrick Holden, Director of the Soil Association, and the Rt. Rev. Richard Chartres Bishop of London; and three by Marcus Cornish of the late Dame Miriam Rothschild, Dr Vandana Shiva, the Indian environmental activist, and the late Dr Kathleen Raine, poet and scholar.

Some busts are positioned over the entrance but others can be spotted further along, on top of the wall, just visible under the tree canopies. A beautiful stone carving runs up each side of this gateway and depicts twining plants with flowers, fruits, a mole, a mouse, a mushroom, birds and other wonderful natural details. It expresses Highgrove's symbiotic relationship with Nature and was created by students from The Prince's Institute of Architecture, with each student carving a block of the overall design.

Beside the entrance, a small patch of long grass and wild flowers sit among the border, which is otherwise packed with lush ferns. This is the grave for Tigga, the much-loved Jack Russell who belonged to Prince Charles and would accompany him on his regular walks around the garden. In the wall is a touching stone carving of her snoozing form created by Marcus Cornish.

One of the most inspiring vistas in this garden is the one that ends with a statue of Diana, Goddess of Hunting. It stands in front of a high yew backdrop that reiterates the ogee arch, cleverly picking up on the shape of the door and frame at the opposite end.

OPPOSITE PAGE

TOP Repeated clusters of *Salvia
nemorosa* 'Caradonna' are punctuated
by white delphiniums and alliums.

LEFT The parallel ornamental
borders that bisect the Kitchen
Garden are at their peak now.

CENTRE
*Delphinium* 'Blue Dawn'

RIGHT
*Allium christophii*

# Kitchen Garden

The Kitchen Garden is one of the most sensational and beautiful gardens at Highgrove in late May and June. Although it is predominantly a productive space there are many ornamental plants and structures within its walls too. The central herbaceous borders full of blues, pinks and purples and the ornamental planting that is intermingled with the fruit trees around the bases of the walls pull in beneficial insects and add to the ambience. The inclusion of flowers for decoration, the strong design and the organic nature are all contributory factors that make this one of the finest kitchen gardens in the country.

The central metal tunnel which dissects the garden from east to west has espaliered apple trees trained over it, which drip pale pink blossom in May and as you stroll slowly down, it seems to release the mouth-watering fragrance of sweet apples. This intoxicating smell will fool you; it hangs in the air when the arch is laden with apples and visitors frequently comment on the heavily scented 'apples' grown here. However, the fragrance comes from lower down, from a line of the sweet briar rose (*Rosa rubiginosa*) that was planted along each side. This species of rose has sweet-smelling foliage and its quite definitely apple-tinged aroma increases in intensity after rain and when the plant is developing new growth. In Spring the walkway is lined by pale, creamy yellow primroses and hellebores which are enchanting in the months when the archway is more sparsely covered.

Other linear plantings create strong patterns within this geometrically defined space. Apple trees, planted just two metres apart, line the internal mellow, brick-paved paths of the two sets of four rectangular beds. These were part of the original Kitchen Garden plan and as they are quite vigorous, they are heavily pruned each year into a perfect goblet shape to reduce shade levels and to prevent their root run interfering with the vegetables within the squares. Some of these well-established trees have dramatic orange lichen on their trunks – this is not harmful, but it is a sign that they are past their more vigorous phase of growth. Lining the beds themselves at ankle height are low hedges of germander, *Teucrium × lucidrys*. This old-fashioned aromatic plant has leaves that are glossy green on top and a matt pale grey-green below and bears masses of

pinky-purple flowers at this time of year. The bees love working the many flowers produced by the thousands of plants that form the extensive run of herbal hedging. Previously dwarf box hedging lined these beds. This plant was an essential part of The Prince's scheme, as the clean, bold lines it produces looked fantastic all year round and its formality contrasted with the more business-like beauty of the cabbages and calabrese. Unfortunately, box blight, a fungal disease, took hold and as fungicides are not an option, the box hedge had to go. The teucrium hedge, which required the planting of 3,000 plants in January 2008, has a more informal look, and more so as it is allowed to flower.

Another special sight that must not be missed now is that of the four arbours, because the roses that entwine them look superb in full swing. The roses and climbers used here were selected 'so that two arbours were in flower at the same time and sometimes all four would be in flower at once'. These arbours are exuberant in their colour and foliage, transforming quickly after a severe pruning and tying, which takes place in April.

The roses that grace these elegant features are 'Paul's Himalayan Musk', a small, dainty climbing rose, which produces soft pink flowers, 'Seagull', a white, single-flowering variety, 'Climbing Pompon de Paris' which bears exquisite, small, pink flowers in April and then again later in the Summer, 'Albertine', one of Prince Charles's favourites, which offers one flush of pink flowers, 'Emily Gray', a once-flowering yellow variety, 'Adélaide d'Orléans', with one flush of creamy pink flowers and 'Sander's White Rambler', a once-flowering white. Added into this mix are white and purple wisterias, honeysuckles and *Clematis montana*.

Centrally placed underneath each arbour is a pot containing a large evergreen rhododendron. In July, this plant is swapped for a hydrangea and the rhododendron is put to one side for another year in the Kitchen Garden until The Prince thinks it will be large enough to create impact in the Arboretum. A younger, smaller specimen will then be brought in to take its place.

The mixed border is at its peak now, with an intensity of colour and flowers that is magnetising. In early April it bursts into life with masses of hyacinths in pale pink, mid-blue and dark purple, which fill the air with scent. The colour theme here is The Prince's favourite palette, a matrix

of dusky pinks, strong blues and purples forming generous swathes, which line the gravel path and run back to the row of charismatic old apple trees that flank the borders.

The main season of interest is early to mid-Summer, when the stars of the show are three large groups of delphiniums and three groups of echinacea. The delphiniums are all Elatum hybrids, which are generally easier to grow and longer living than other hybrids, and can form fabulous three-metre towers of blue, white and purple, from 'Blue Dawn', 'White Ruffles' and 'Chelsea Star'. The *Echinacea* chosen is 'bressingham hybrid', which will grow in excess of a metre high in this good, rich soil. The cone flower, as it is commonly known, blooms from June right through to Autumn with its appealing orange bobbly centres and contrasting reddish-purple fluorescent petals.

The blue colour spectrum is highlighted with *Iris sibirica*, with its velvety violet flowers, and *Salvia nemorosa* 'Caradonna' which, unlike the iris, goes on and on from now until October. *Geranium* 'Rozanne' is a purply blue, sterile cranesbill, which means it flowers for far longer – for several months from now until Autumn. *Aquilegia vulgaris* 'Clementine Salmon Rose', with its fluffy, pale salmon-pink flowers with pale yellow centres adds a softer tone to the mix.

Bulbs puncture the heady mass of colour, pushing up through their herbaceous bedfellows. *Lilium martagon* is a species lily that produces many flowers – 12 or so per stem – and looks supremely elegant in tall clumps under the old apple trees. These curious flowers vary from a muted dark maroon through mauve to white in colour and will grow in excess of 1.2 metres high when happy in sun or even in shadier spots. As an added bonus, in the Autumn their seed heads form attractive silhouettes that look beautiful dusted with dew or a layer of frost.

Baby's Breath – *Gypsophila paniculata* 'Festival White' and *G.* 'Festival Pink' – are frothy plants that will flower from May to October with a bit of dead heading in between. Their tiny flowers are produced in profusion and are ever popular both outside and when brought inside to add freshness and charm to an arrangement. All these ornamentals undoubtedly add to the ambience, but they also lure lots of beneficial insects, such as hoverflies, bees, wasps and butterflies.

BELOW The straight lines of the Kitchen Garden are heavily disguised by lush planting in June, with no two beds alike.

RIGHT and OVERLEAF The long-flowering *Rosa* 'Raubritter' dangles in the water of the central dunking pool; its blooms are rounded, cupped, and full of old rose character.

Roses surround this garden; their ephemeral beauty, scent and ebullience is so quintessentially part of an English walled garden that it would be strange if they were absent. The roses, all organically grown, have to look reasonably healthy; if they are miffy and succumb regularly to blackspot and mildew then they must be removed. This is the fate that befell *R*, 'Leverkusen'. This rose could not be spared, because an important part of organic growing, be it vegetables or ornamentals, is to choose strong, healthy varieties so that you are not harbouring sources of disease and infection.

Currently, *Rosa mundi* is the most striking old rose whose semi-double flowers sport stripes of pink and white on a crimson magenta background. It is said to be named after Fair Rosamund who was the mistress of Henry II in the twelfth century. This charming rose has one glorious flowering and at Highgrove it is grown in the diagonally shaped arrangement under the apple trees.

Flavour and looks combine when sweet peas and runner beans ramble over tunnels of hazel and willow that stride over the diagonal paths by the two damson trees. While the beans are being harvested the spent sweet pea flowers are removed to ensure more appear and the garden enjoys a long season of fragrance and colour. All the ties for these tunnels are made from recyclable materials which help these structures blend in well with their natural environment. The hazel and willow from the tunnels are either reused the following year or chipped and used as mulch.

Another much-visited patch of this garden now is the asparagus beds. These were planted 15 to 20 years ago and have been known in good years to produce a thousand spears of this sought-after delicacy, which is a firm royal favourite. Soon a new patch will have to be established, which usually means waiting three long years until they can be harvested. Some new asparagus plants have recently been put in around one of the arbours; the choice of varieties will ensure a long cropping season, starting with 'Gijnlim', an early season, all-male variety with medium thick spears, 'Arianne F1', which produces high yields of thick spears early in the season, 'Backlim' a thick-speared, late male variety, and 'Pacific Purple' which produces thick, purple, sweet and tender spears. There is a strict rule at Highgrove that no picking takes place after 20 June, which enables the plant to rest and build up reserves for the following year.

Like the beds, the wheelbarrow is full to bursting every week too, overflowing with lettuce, perhaps a few early new potatoes, young beetroot, small, sweet carrots, rhubarb, broad beans, peas and spinach as well as big bundles of asparagus, all of which the royal chefs will cook to perfection. As any allotmenteer or vegetable gardener knows, the beauty of home-grown produce is the flavour and freshness that they possess, which makes it immensely satisfying for any cook to work with such choice raw ingredients.

*Delphinium*
'Faust'

# JULY

'The roses are in full bloom – one of my favourites being 'Jude the Obscure' which grows up the Indian Gate. On the Terrace the lady's mantle forms a carpet of pale yellow tufts interspersed with all the Mediterranean plants growing in the cracks between the paving. The marjoram is in flower and if there is hot sunshine it is covered with shifting, swirling clouds of bumble bees and butterflies – small coppers, peacocks, meadow browns and cabbage whites. In the Kitchen Garden the central borders are at their best and I gaze in admiration at the clumps of seven-foot tall purple, blue and white delphiniums holding their heads high at the back of the borders. The excitement of all the new vegetables is at its height – the tiny, rare purple carrots being the best – and then suddenly there is a mass of strawberries, raspberries and gooseberries.The Carpet Garden now comes into its own, just as the Meadow becomes overgrown and the grass turns brown. The Front Drive, however, is a mass of mauve scabious, purple knapweed, yellow hypericum and sweet-scented Lady's bedstraw that have taken up residence in this area and act as a floral fuel station for fluttering flotillas of butterflies and droning squadrons of bees.'

IN THE HEAT OF THE SUMMER, A VISIT TO the Carpet Garden is rather like stepping into an exotic, foreign location as you are greeted by bold hot colours, heady perfumes and gently trickling rills and fountains. The Meadow, on the other hand, could not look more English at this time of year; cut down and bleached with the hay removed, ready to be grazed a little later by the fine Lleyn sheep that roam The Prince's land. The Lawns, or 'mown green spaces' as they are called, look verdant though, full of herbs which keep them green and thick. As the sun rises high in the sky and the temperatures with it, the Winterbourne Garden provides welcome shade as well as magnificent late-Summer colour just as some other planting begins to go over and redirects its energies into producing seeds for another generation.

PREVIOUS The red *Rosa* 'Highgrove' and pink *R.* 'Home Sweet Home' are trained along the self-sown oak saplings.

RIGHT Nasturtiums are beginning to flower on the wigwam in the Terrace Garden; the lime-yellow *Alchemilla* is cut back later to prolong flowering.

# The 'Lawn'

His Royal Highness is famous for his wildflower meadows and also, though perhaps to a lesser extent, for his 'mown green spaces'. The 'mown green spaces' are not called lawns at Highgrove because grass is not the dominant plant in these sections – the ground is full of myriad herbs too. These green spaces are, however, invariably green and beautifully striped, but also teeming with many wild flowers. 'I love moss, too,' Prince Charles admits. 'Sometimes I think I would like to leave some more patches of lawn to grow as I can see so many wild flowers appearing in them. It would be quite fun to create a patchwork quilt of mown and unmown grass and just leave a bit unmown and see what grows.' The deliberate lack of herbicide use and fertiliser application in line with the organic gardening approach ensures greater plant diversity, which makes these areas more interesting to visitors but also to butterflies, bees and other insects that visit in increasing numbers.

The perfect, flat mown spaces are punctuated with highlights. Four sturdy, fine, lichen-covered stone benches are spaced against the yew hedge, two on each side. Each bench is flanked by two Greek urns planted with hydrangeas (*H. paniculata*) and loose clumps of moon daisies (*Leucanthemum vulgare*) jostle at the base, their almost iridescent white flowers strident against the dark yew so that they appear to glow in the twilight – hence their common name. Although June is the month for the

moon daisy – as legend has it, it naturally flowers on Midsummer's day – they will often flower longer, especially if they are dead headed regularly.

The other elements which gives emphasis to these four classically designed stone seats are the two pairs of Japanese flowering crab apple (*Malus floribunda*) that grow on each side. These are used to create more intimately scaled places to sit; somewhere to relax and appreciate their magnificent Spring blossom. These four small 'bowers' are set in an otherwise large, fairly open, but beautiful and simple space.

The vast majority of grass on the 'lawn' is mown. A few larger patches have been left untended in order to furnish the ground below the larger trees – some of which were here when His Royal Highness moved to Highgrove. These grasses are now long and the gentle, beautifully flowering stems sway in the breeze, catching the light and rippling in waves like the sea.

There is a massive, majestic plane tree in the far left-hand corner away from the house. There is also a mature Irish yew, which has become fairly wide with age as these

LEFT Colourful lupins are on display in the Buttress Garden (at the end of the Cottage Garden); this area is used to experiment with colour schemes.

ABOVE Four Italian statues, depicting the four seasons, sit between the gaps of each set of hornbeams on the Lawn.

ABOVE Herbs are encouraged on the 'mown green spaces', which help keep the areas green in dry summers.

ABOVE RIGHT Several specimens of yew have been topiarised into eccentric shapes, including within a back-to-back seat.

fastigiated yews tend to do. A corresponding plane has been planted more recently on the opposite side, with a yew pruned back to restore it. They are neighbours to a wonderful old, lichen-spotted *Magnolia × soulangeana*, which now spreads over four metres or more. Sometimes as early as late May the huge vase-shaped flowers will make an appearance, which are white with a central carmine-coloured stripe. Some specimen beeches are to be found here too, planted in the days after Prince Charles first arrived and now, at an age of 30 years or so, they are significant, sizeable and healthy specimens.

The 'lawns' here at Highgrove are richer habitats than those that boast a conventional bowling green finish; they are not weeded, sprayed, aerated or fertilised like traditional swards. The main lawns are cut with a cylinder mower and the cuttings are removed and composted, thus adding regular amounts of vital bulk to the heaving heaps of organic matter that feed the rest of the garden. As a result, the lawns stay a lush green even when there is a drought. Before, when the lawns were more grass and fewer herbs, they regularly used to turn khaki-coloured in dry Summers. The rich tapestry of herbs and many different grasses used here has also helped to combat this unsightly problem. Plants such as self-heal (*Prunella vulgaris*), thymes, daisies

and many more have gradually colonised the space and a wider range of grasses have also established and thrived. All these plants are more tolerant of drought and so will thrive even in the hottest, driest Summers.

The pleached hornbeams that form beautiful, high rectangular blocks on either side of the Thyme Walk were planted in around 1987. These trees are important pieces of green architecture that give strength to the strong vista that runs out to the Dovecote. Even in Winter, their twig and branch structure provides a sharp, welcome presence. In 1989, Roy Strong sourced four fine classical statues (which represent the four seasons) from Italy. These now sit in the gaps between the sets of hornbeams and they lift the whole garden, making it very much fit for a king.

There are a few fine wood benches, which are situated in the thyme walk and look over the lawns. His Royal Highness is extremely interested in the Platonic solids and so he asked Stephen Florence to design four benches, each incorporating one of them on their backrest. Earth, Fire, Air, Water are featured; the fifth solid, the Cosmos, is marked by a carved stone pentagon which in fact is the top of a dodecahedron that is set into the middle of the Thyme Walk. If you stand on this stone and look at the benches, each one is in line with one of the four statues.

# Meadow

Since the now world-famous Wildflower Meadows were started at Highgrove in the early Eighties, they have gradually increased in richness and diversity. This has happened as a result of careful nurturing and a honing of the techniques used to maintain the Meadows. Nothing is set in stone, though, and every method used is subject to change if the conditions dictate.

It is often forgotten that grass is a rich source of pollen, which is an important food for bees, insects, spiders and many other arthropods, but equally bee-friendly are the lime trees. The avenue of red-twigged limes, *Tilia platyphyllos* 'Rubra', is buzzing with bees at this time of year, which work the small, fragrant, yellowish-white flowers which hang in drooping clusters and can be picked and dried for tea. These limes have a natural, semi-erect habit, but every few years the lower limbs are lifted to encourage the typical Gothic-shaped arch formed by the lower branches, which beautifully frame the view to the Dovecote. The trees for the Lime Avenue were a gift from the Men of Trees; each branch gave a tree, and there are 36 trees in all. Limes make ideal avenue trees because they establish quickly on brashy lime soils far quicker than many other good avenue options, such as oak, chestnut and beech.

Towards the end of July the majority of wild flowers and grasses have set seed and the Meadow starts to appear bleached and slightly tired. However, before the Meadow is cut, the long grass is brush harvested to collect the seed. This is done with a machine that combs the grass, rolling the stems over a cylinder and so collecting tiny bits of stalk and seed into a reservoir. The collected seed is then laid out for a day on a tarpaulin so that all the insects can crawl out, and then left to dry for a week or more before it is winnowed. Winnowing involves throwing it in the air with a sieve to remove unwanted bits of stalk and undesirable seeds, particularly those of cow parsley, which are conveniently large. The seed is then dried and stored ready to use in regenerating new areas. Many wild flowers germinate

PREVIOUS The Wildflower Meadow
is a triumph and every year new
plants are establishing themselves.

RIGHT In August, the Meadow is
cut, often with Austrian scythes.

better if the seed is fresh, so harvesting your own means
you know its vital statistics – its source and age.

Between the end of July and beginning of August,
the Highgrove team set about the task of cutting the
Meadow. Often now, as the various areas are becoming
rich in different species, cutting is done over a period of
time, not in one go, to ensure that valuable seed is spread
before the plants are removed and so wildlife can adapt
to the shock.

The way in which cutting is carried out varies according
to the weather and the condition of the Meadow. In
unusually wet Summers, as occurred in 2012, the tall sward
stayed quite thick and green, whereas in more normal
years the base of the grass is yellow, dry and quite thin
by July. When the Meadow is lush it is not easy for the
horse-drawn mower to cut it – it is just too thick for the
blades – and so a side-mounted mower pulled by a quad
bike will be used.

Scything of meadows is now coming back into vogue.
The old-fashioned scythes that were used in Britain until
quite recently are quite difficult to use, as they are long
(some find them dauntingly huge) and not so easy to work
effectively. However, scything using the Austrian-designed
scythe (a Schrockenflux scythe, which has a blade just
60 centimetres long or so and a handle length selected to
fit the user's body dimensions), is becoming increasingly
popular. These scythes are made by the same company
that made them in the 1540s and many find that using
them 'relaxes the mind and attunes the body', as opposed
to doing battle with a noisy trimmer. The rhythmic action
involves stopping to sharpen the blade at ten-minute
intervals to keep a sharp edge. The necessary pauses in
your scything action have big benefits to your body, too;
at Highgrove there are parties of scything enthusiasts who
enjoy coming to scythe the Meadow as it gives them highly
satisfying and gentle exercise in a stunning environment.

After the Meadow is cut, the hay is left to dry and then
it is baled up, removed and fed to livestock. The Meadow
is usually grazed after it is cut. Obviously the yew hedges
(which bear highly toxic berries and foliage) and the
Meadow trees are vulnerable to the animals, and vice versa,
so they are back fenced where necessary with temporary
electric fences. Prince Charles discovered more recently
that Shropshire sheep, which can be used to graze orchards
and conifer plantations, do not eat mature bark from older
trees. They might nibble on any tasty young leaves that are
within reach, but they do not stand on their hind legs to
do so as many breeds will, and so do not attack the trunks.

When these sheep are well managed and not over-
stocked they are superb, enabling you to double-crop an
area, for example by having fruit trees or conifers and sheep
on the same piece of land. Before Prince Charles realised
this, he had chosen beautiful Black Hebridean sheep,
because they are a rare breed, as well as white Welsh Lleyn
sheep. At Highgrove the sheep are brought in to graze the
Meadow from around mid-August to October. Sheep are
very tight grazers and will nibble the sward down to give a
very close 'buzz' cut, unlike cattle, who graze by wrapping
their tongues around the grass, which inevitably leaves a
longer finish.

The sheep, with their small hooves, gently tread the
surface, which helps the fallen wild flower seeds come into
contact with the soil. The Meadow is a constantly evolving
space, and the sheep play a part in this, but The Prince also
increases diversity by slot seeding, using plug plants, and
also scattering green hay complete with its fresh seeds as
the Meadow moves into its Autumnal phase. Through such
management yellow rattle populations have increased,
helping to weaken the grass and so allowing the numbers
of wild flowers to increase.

The seasonal and yearly changes within the Meadow
are all keenly observed by The Prince and Head Gardener,
and as the space becomes more rich, many more gardeners
become intrigued. Meadows are highly dynamic as they
can fill a square foot or several acres; each year they have
the potential to become more fascinating and every
year is different.

# Transylvanian Meadow

There is a large area of meadow directly in front of the Orchard Room, which has a closer mown band of grass around its edge with several specimen trees scattered too – some interesting beech trees and a lovely mature *Clerodendron* that were rescued from a building site in Tetbury.

At first glance you might think that it is just another of Highgrove's wildflower-rich areas; there are buttercups, purple clovers and, among the grasses, many low herbaceous plants. This, however, is an experimental Transylvanian Meadow, and it has a fascinating story behind it.

As is the case with any great historical garden, Highgrove is continually changing and evolving. Most recently, His Royal Highness was inspired by his journeys to Transylvania, where he was bowled over by the country's beautiful untouched pastures.

When Prince Charles first visited Transylvania in 1998 he said, 'I was totally overwhelmed by its unique beauty and its extraordinarily rich heritage.' Since then he has made many repeated visits to try to conserve its landscape. It is, apparently, the last corner of Europe that has been relatively untouched and so its environment is unique.

'I have been battling for years to try to save their unique wildflower meadows because they are probably what this country would have looked like 800 years ago in terms of wild flowers. It's because they have had this traditional system of farming, grazing and cutting hay for hundreds and hundreds of years and this has produced a unique landscape. The flora and insect life and butterflies are as England would have been'.

His Royal Highness initially became aware of the destruction of these meadows because the area in Romania where his great- great-grandmother, Countess Rhédey von Kis-Rhéde came from, was threatened with destruction from Ceausescu. He was extremely concerned that these meadows would suffer the fate of their British counterparts.

In the UK, just 1 per cent of the wildflower-rich meadows of the 1940s have survived. This is due to the use of herbicides, fertilisers and loss of permanent pasture that are a part of modern agricultural practices. Now, in

Transylvania, an increasingly progressive modernisation of agriculture is causing large areas of the wildflower-rich pastures to disappear in the same way. Prince Charles realises the huge international importance of these threatened meadows, as they represent a living model of how traditional farming with its associated rich bio-diversity could be a model to restore habitat diversity in Europe. These meadows have low-stocking densities of animals and low inputs of fertilisers and herbicides and as such they are a rich legacy for us to learn from.

In 2008 The Prince purchased a property in the village of Zalánpatak, which was founded four centuries ago by the Kalnoky family. This house has some forest and extensive flower meadows, which are characterised by a huge variety of native plants. As part of his plan to preserve the diversity of these magical meadows, these are now maintained in the traditional way.

Encouraged by his Transylvanian meadows, Prince Charles decided to try to replicate one at Highgrove in 2010. As the area of grass in front of the Orchard Room is fairly self-contained, it was decided that this area would be the perfect place to do this. Many of the flowers in Transylvanian meadows would have been native to Britain too, so wildflower seed was taken from barn floor sweepings in Transylvania and seeded at Highgrove. Invasive species that could escape and cause problems were left out of the mix, as were plants which could breed with British genetic material and cause confusion amongst our local populations.

The range of wild flowers that have been sown there include the beautiful blue-flowered meadow clary (*Salvia pratensis*), which many gardeners grow here in more cultivated parts of their gardens, usually as a border plant or rising up through gravel. Sainfoin (*Onobrychis*) is a Transylvanian variant of our common silage or hay crop and has dark-veined pink flowers. A charming yellow rock rose (*Helianthemum nummularium*) is well known to gardeners too and the crown vetch (*Coronilla varia*) and the pink pea flower (*Lathyrus tuberosus*) are both colourful plants regularly seen in Transylvanian meadows. Hopefully they will become more visible at Highgrove too as this little piece of Transylvania takes root in a corner of Britain.

# Carpet Garden

The Carpet Garden is an exquisite site, perhaps all the more so due to the sharp contrast of entering from a Cotswold orchard. This garden is inspired by an original sketch by His Royal Highness, based on a Turkish carpet. The sketch was given to Emma Clark, who is an expert on Islamic gardens and their symbolism, and she developed the final design for the RHS Chelsea Flower Show, along with Khaled Azzam.

Prince Charles explains, 'After gazing for many years at the patterns and colours of one of the small Turkish carpets in my room at Highgrove, I couldn't help feeling what fun it would be to use those patterns and colours to create a theme for a garden. The challenge would be to see if you could almost create the effect of being within the carpet.

'I have a particular fascination for the ancient geometric principles of Islamic art and architecture, and for this reason I set up the Visual Islamic and Traditional Arts programme at my foundation in Shoreditch, headed by Dr Khaled Azzam. Dr Assam has worked very closely with Mike Miller of Clifton Nurseries to bring life to my original and rather rudimentary ideas for the garden and I am enormously grateful to them. They have done a wonderful job in making sure the geometry worked, making sure the

planting worked and in managing to ensure the garden reflected the underlying, harmonious principles.'

The Carpet Garden, sponsored by Porcelanosa in association with *Homes and Gardens*, was a triumph at the RHS Chelsea Flower Show in May 2001, drawing huge crowds and winning a coveted Silver-Gilt medal from the Royal Horticultural Society.

It was the first time that a member of the Royal Family had designed an entry for Chelsea, and this move served to reinforce the public's growing awareness that Prince Charles is fascinated with gardening and design and that gardening had become more than just a hobby.

In the warm red evening light the now mature cork oak trees (*Quercus suber*) cast dappled shade over the strong blues, purples, reds and pinks that dominate the planting palette. Shafts of the pink light accentuate the planting hues so they glow and become more vibrant, making everything seem more three-dimensional. The narrow,

dark green columns of the pencil cypress trees (*Cupressus sempervirens* Stricta Group) have grown above the wall and filled out. Climbers, including roses, clematis, figs and trachelospermums adorn the warm pink rendered walls, breaking up and softening them to add more blues, purples, whites and reds.

More personal touches have been added by The Prince as he has travelled and accreted wonderful 'finds'. Two fine chairs were acquired in India about eight years ago and these have pride of place on the raised plinth by the main doorway. By one of the two central doors on the long sides of the rectangular garden, a quirky, small, carved galloping horse has been inset into the wall, as if providing a place to hang your coat, along with Moorish lanterns, which are scattered around, as well as lime-washed pots. It is a garden that is a small piece of perfection, but one that will no doubt be added to as inspiration strikes on every trip The Prince makes!

LEFT These splendid, decorated wooden doors are painted with bold Saudi Arabian designs.

RIGHT The Prince found this chair (one of two) in India.

BELOW The soft bubbling sounds of the Moroccan-inspired fountain adds calm and authenticity to this hidden, secret garden.

# Winterbourne Garden

Entering the east side of the Winterbourne Garden from the Meadow takes you through a transition that is gentle and charming; the open Meadow gives way to a shadier area replete with groundcover plantings of sweet woodruff, camassias and the occasional fern.

As you make your way into the heart of the Winterbourne Garden, a slightly curving, stepping-stone path takes you into a shadier, higher level. This more intensely planted space has wide, gently curving borders edged with felled tree ferns. Sadly, these beautiful plants could not cope with our sudden swing into cold, long Winters. Now lying on the ground, their trunks are being colonised with plants, giving them a new life and role within this garden.

Dead wood is of immense ecological value, and the tree fern trunks look decorative as an edging, defining the borders in a charming but rustic fashion. Some foxgloves are seeding into these trunks and the silvery toned leaves of *Astelia chathamica* hang over them. A few sturdy tree ferns have survived, though, and their huge, fresh green fronds glint when they are caught by the sun.

The borders are deep here, filled with many low-level generous plantings of shady favourites such as *Pulmonaria* 'Blue Ensign', *Omphaloides Cappadocica* 'Cherry Ingram', and *Tellima grandiflora*. The tellima, or fringe cup, is showing off its spikes of greenish-white flowers at this time of year. Other taller plants are flowering well now too, with several *Cornus kousa* 'Venus' in bloom, and a variety of heavily

scented philadelphus such as *P.* 'Manteau d'Hermine', *P.* 'Snowbelle' and *P.* 'Silberregen'.

Lots of different types of *Hydrangea paniculata* have been added here, including 'Limelight', which, as its name suggests, has blooms from lime green through to white then fading to pink and 'Sundae Fraise', with its ice cream soft pinks and reds. By planting a wide range of at least 15 varieties of paniculate hydrangeas, the colourful flower clusters will start to appear from July and will carry on to October.

The high Kitchen Garden wall is visible from most of the Winterbourne Garden, and walking along the wide gravel path beside it, you see magnificent tall groups of hardy bananas reaching the upper limits of the wall, their giant leaves looking almost translucent as they catch the Summer sun. Near them are Chusan palms, more tree ferns and balsam poplars, either planted in island beds or in a border by the wall. One of the Chusan palms is raised from the seed of the first palm grown outside in England; its parent, now dead, was planted by Queen Victoria in 1851 at Osborne House. Debs Goodenough gave a seedling to Prince Charles when he visited Osborne House, while she was Head Gardener there.

At the eastern end of the garden is a recently created topiary border where a small nursery is a work in progress, intended as a space in which Highgrove's own, homegrown topiary can be produced.

LEFT Some tree ferns survived the harsh Winter of 2010, giving this garden an exotic feel.

ABOVE RIGHT Panicle hydrangeas thrive in this fairly dry, shady site and their white flowers stand out among the rich green foliage.

RIGHT The buttresses in the Winterbourne Garden have been made from reclaimed stonework. They provide a handy bridge to the higher level – for the more agile!

The planting which runs along the bank and down to the edge of the Winterbourne stream is vibrant and tropical in feel. Giant gunnera, or Chilean rhubarb, have now unfurled their huge leaves and are supported by tall prickly stalks which stretch out to two metres long. In early Summer, tiny red flowers appear on its tall, erect spikes, adding to the prehistoric feel of these ancient plants.

Until recently the wall here was covered with ivy and roses. These have been removed now and self-clinging plants such as *Hydrangea anomala* subsp. *petiolaris* and Boston ivy (*Parthenocissus tricuspidata* 'Robusta') run along its length instead. A specimen of *Acradenia frankliniae,* an unusual shrub from the citrus family, has been established. This glossy-leaved evergreen comes from Tasmania and has pretty white flowers in late Spring.

Leaving the garden from its western end, you pass through beautifully detailed, double oak gates designed by Charles Morris. These open out onto a path bordered by serpentine hedges, one end of which leads towards the Sundial Garden and the other into the Azalea Walk.

# Stumpery

In mid-Summer, the Stumpery is in full leaf and the clothed mounds and lush foliage make this sylvan space seem easily large enough for you to lose your bearings within its concealed boundaries. It is a far cry from the cold, windswept space punctuated with sycamores and smothered with a dense weedy undergrowth of nettles and brambles that was here when The Prince arrived.

In 2002 nine large sycamores that had been damaged by grey squirrels had to be removed. The space was immediately consumed by light, which in turn opened it up to more planning and planting. Once again, Prince Charles called in the Bannermans and together they decided to increase and develop the Stumpery, which had started to take its current form in 1996.

Originally there had been a depression some way behind the East Temple, so it was agreed that they should utilise this dip and create a dynamic body of water there to enhance the atmosphere of the space. Water is wonderful for bouncing light into an area, adding humidity and creating interest, and now, as you enter the Stumpery from the walk through the meadow, you are immediately aware of a beautiful, naturally shaped pool. In the centre of this lies a huge, magnificent stone edifice, out of which grows a wonderful, monstrously lush gunnera.

The mammoth and artfully arranged stone tower that dominates the pool is just over two metres high and a similar width. It is formed by wonderful, holey pieces of grotto-type rock or spugna (which came from Barcelona) that are positioned on the top and cascade down the sides. It appears to be supported with curious pieces of dressed and carved stone on the vertices, which were salvaged from Hereford Cathedral. There are large stone clamshells built within the stonework, too, which are also recycled pieces, having come from Edward VII's garden at Sandringham. The middle of the structure is filled with compost, which explains the lavish proportions of the gunnera growing on top, arcing out like a fountain of water.

Water splashes down the whole structure and adds to the moody, mystical atmosphere of the Stumpery, also making it a magnet for countless wildlife. Mallards and moorhens have nested on top of the fountain, rearing their broods safely out of the reach of predatory foxes. Not surprisingly, given the numbers of water fowl that pop in, you may see a light shimmer of lime-green duck weed

*Gunnera manicata* looks magnificent
atop the two-metre-high stone tower.

from time to time. The duck weed is periodically cleared with a net and barley straw extract is added to control the blanket weed, which is a natural, organic method of control.

On one bank, there are two cranes made from recycled car parts, which seem so lifelike they can almost be confused with the real thing, and were a gift from a Zimbabwean relation of one of the gardeners.

In order to make the Stumpery more accessible for visitors and to increase its potential, more of the surrounding woodland was brought in. The soil from the excavation of the pool and from the Carpet Garden, which was being installed at this time, amounted to some 200 tons, and was used to form more low, heavily planted mounds, which were then encrusted with stumps to reinforce the physical separation from the outside world.

New paths were designed to allow visitors to wander by, using ammonite fossils – a traditional method of paving that has been employed since medieval times. Alongside the gently curving ammonite paths, small, reclaimed stones were laid on end and made to look like well-worn, dry-stone walling on its side. The paths are flanked by stumps and ferns, which guide you through the lush and beautiful woodland plantings, and so in July the space seems much larger than it feels in the Winter.

Throughout the Stumpery, the planting is laid out in many tiers, from the vast, high canopies of trees, down to a layer of shrubs and finally a prolific lower storey of groundcover plants and bulbs. Certain favourite plants, such as *Philadelphus coronarius* 'Aureus' (golden-leaved mock orange) are planted either as specimens or in groups

BELOW Standing stones of vertical slate are planted along one of the pathways in the Stumpery, guiding visitors through the woodland plantings.

RIGHT In high Summer, the Stumpery transforms as the vegetation fills out, creating a lush carpet.

of three, with around 30 or so in total. At this time of year their sweet-smelling perfume wafts and lingers in this beautifully sheltered space and their brighter hue looks as though they are bouncing shafts of light from their leaves, lifting the dark greens of their neighbours. Another favourite is *Philadelphus × purpureomaculatus*, which has arching stems and exquisite, purple-stained, fragrant white blossoms.

The Prince of Wales is the holder of the National Collection of Hostas (large- and giant-leaved section), and so at Highgrove, particularly the Stumpery, you will find a wide variety – clothing the banks and edging the curving paths, often mixed with ferns so as not to appear too dominant. The first hosta to appear in Spring is invariably *Hosta* 'Chinese Sunrise'; this is not part of the National Collection as it has small leaves, but it is valued here as its light green-golden leaves lift the planting scheme on drab days.

By late June and early July, the hostas are looking dramatic – their bold, full leaves look almost surreal and are also surprisingly undamaged by slugs. The lack of holes gives rise to the most often asked question by visitors, 'How are they so perfect when no slug pellets are ever used?' No one is totally sure why; the adjacent meadow has a healthy population of slugs, but one theory is that while slugs and snails like eating the leaves they don't actually like living among the hosta plants.

There is a phenomenal bird population at Highgrove, especially of thrushes, as well as heaving communities of frogs, toads and newts (attracted by the pool), and slow worms, all of which greedily gobble up slugs. It is not uncommon to see and hear a thrush bashing a snail shell on a rock just a stone's throw from a visitor's heel. Grass snakes (harmless and quite beautiful) also live in the damp spaces around the pool, and slugs are quite a delicacy for them too. The hostas are not completely ignored by the wildlife, though, as rabbits and pheasants do have a penchant for pecking or chewing on unfurling leaves – especially in a dry Spring when they relish the moisture they are able to find on offer.

Mophead hydrangea
*Hydrangea macrophylla*

# AUGUST

'This can be a difficult time to maintain interest and colour in the garden. Things have 'gone over the top', gone to seed and look worn at the edges. Heavy reliance is placed on strategically sited hydrangeas with their pink, blue, purple (if you are lucky and have the right soil!) and white confections catching shafts of sunlight between the trees. In the Meadow the orchids have set their seed and the hay can be cut in stages using a combination of the horse-drawn cutter (easier to manoeuvre round the trees and less damaging to soft ground) and enthusiastic volunteers from the British Scything Society. Yes, it exists, and I was overjoyed when I found out about it; so now ten men – and women – come to mow the Meadow! On the Terrace and in the Kitchen Garden, the good old nasturtiums are spilling over pots, paths and paving and provide wonderful dollops of 'hot' colours in the dog days of Summer. I came across a spectacularly dark red nasturtium last year called 'Empress of India', which adds a certain distinction to its surroundings …'

## Lily Pool Garden

MANY GARDENS MAY START TO FADE IN August as Summer inexorably heads into Autumn, but the landscape at Highgrove now takes on a new lease of life. The clear, cool water in the Lily Pool Garden is studded with delicately fragrant lilies nestled among glossy lily pads, beckoning visitors to sit beside it and enjoy its tranquillity. The shadier spaces, such as the Arboretum and Stumpery, promise respite from hot August days, but also offer their own golden glow with the superb bright leaves of the golden philadelphus (*Philadelphus coronarius* 'Aureus') and the bright blooms of the paniculate and other hydrangeas lighten the shade. The ancient Parkland with its blond grass and mature trees with typical, almost black-green canopies of high Summer is studded with sleek, contented grazing cattle, while the Carpet Garden ramps up into top gear as the roses burst into their second flush, the pelargoniums increase in vibrance and vigour and the Russian sage (*Perovskia atriplicifolia*) and phlox explode with colour.

If you step down the shallow stone step to the water's edge in the heat of an August day, you will see the very tiny, newly planted lilies. The lilies that grow here are all scented varieties; *Nymphaea* 'Yul Ling' bears deep pink flowers, *N.* 'Rosy Morn' softer, strawberry coloured ones, *N. mexicana* and *odorata* offers a burst of yellow and *N.* 'White Sultan' is, predictably, white. Each has also been selected because it is of low or medium vigour, so that none will dominate or cover too much of the water.

The air in this semi-enclosed, restful space is filled with other scents, too. Yellow roses, golden origanum, artemesias, lavender and thyme are interspersed with earlier flowering scented plants such as golden philadelphus and daphne. The colour scheme of the planting here was changed in 2012 when it was decided to go for a restful and harmonious blue and yellow scheme. Enhancing the colour are four pink cherries, *Prunus* 'Pink Perfection', one positioned on each side of the two entrances.

These compact trees with their ascending branches are covered with drooping clusters of light pink flowers in late Spring.

There are other interesting details here too to keep you seated to enjoy the scene. Around the pool are four stone pots that are decorated with fruits around their vertical sides and planted up with neatly clipped pyramids of box. Lichens grow on two of the pots, which add an attractive tinge and texture to its surface. The paving of the garden is an informal mix of bricks, stone setts and stone slabs, which has been softened by filling the wide joints with clusters of *Alchemilla mollis*, thymes, and stonecrops to name but a few of the plants.

This is an extraordinary garden of contrasts – both restful and energising. The sound and sight of the immaculately detailed water lifts your spirits and the aroma from the sun-baked lavenders is soothing, as are the restful proportions of the space. Yet these calming elements contrast with the life and vitality conveyed by the intriguing gladiator and the drama of the two dominant vistas running from west to east. In Highgrove, Prince Charles wanted to create a garden to 'warm the heart, feed the soul and delight the eye'. The Lily Pool garden is just one small part of this important garden, but it goes a long way towards illustrating just how the garden at Highgrove works on so many levels.

BELOW The Borghese Gladiator
statue stands between the Lily Pool
Garden and Lime Avenue.

RIGHT The view from the Lily Pool
Garden up towards the Thyme Walk
shows varying colours of green and
gold in the heat of Summer.

# Arboretum

When you enter the cool expanse of the Arboretum and escape the high August sun, you are greeted with a refreshing mix of lime, emerald and bottle greens. The plants have the fertile, deep soil in this section of the garden to thank for this, combined with the protective canopy above that keeps everything growing on the ground beautifully fresh and green. The evergreens, mainly yew, box, rhododendrons and camellias, combine to create a serene feel, while the beguiling hydrangeas, mainly lace caps, mop heads and *Hydrangea aspera*, add to the tranquillity with their restful late-season shades.

Shapely deciduous groups of these fine shrubs with flowers of mauves, pale limes, whites and blue are positioned near the edges of the rides and paths. These plantings are quite recent; the Arboretum was originally planned for a Spring and Autumn colour surge, but as the collection of trees is so fascinating and the arrangement so strong, a decision was later made by His Royal Highness to pull colour through into the Summer months too.

As you look up the wide, grassy ride towards the 'Daughters of Odessa' bronze statue from the ha-ha, the route is lined with a selection of azaleas, all of which have sweetly scented flowers in Spring, followed by excellent colours of deep fiery reds and purples.

Along the rides throughout the Arboretum, rows of trees are planted on a radius, as opposed to a grid of straight lines (as done in forestry plantings) so to keep the feel soft and organic. The acers along the walkways form open, multi-stemmed small trees, which look shapely – especially as their branches are highlighted with their delicate foliage.

Underneath, a floor of grasses, ferns and natives such as the sweet woodruff (*Galium odoratum*), creeping buttercup and dog's mercury (*Mercurialis perennis*) has carpeted the ground, covering over the Spring bulbs that have long since

The walkways in the Arboretum are lined with groups of acers, which have had formative pruning over the years.

retired underground. The main grassy rides are mown and the longer areas are selectively trimmed a few times a year, but not until the foliage from the bulbs has died down, letting the bulbs gain the nutrients provided by the foliage to ensure a good performance the following Spring.

The basic layout of the Arboretum was briefed by Prince Charles, designed by John White, and was based around Robert Holford's principles. Robert Holford created Westonbirt Arboretum, and one of his main principles was 'to create variety without confusion, [to create] informality and picturesqueness'. The planning of any garden's layout is key, but with an arboretum that develops over an extremely long time frame, establishing the principles that will govern its management and development over the years is crucial.

Another of Holford's principles was not to have a pre-planting plan set in stone, but to keep options open in order to be able to extend the design to every stage of the Arboretum's development. Over the years Prince Charles has heeded this advice, selecting and adding his favourite trees, shrubs and bulbs and other elements while still loosely adhering to the concept design.

In order to have an expanse of beautiful Autumn colours, it was decided that along one of the paths deviating from the main circuitous route around the Arboretum, the trees and shrubs planted should be predominantly those that have Autumn interest. A few beeches (for Prince Charles's National Collection), were also planned to go here, including *Fagus sylvatica* 'Quercifolia', *F.s.* 'Ansorgei', and *F. s.* 'Dawyck' (a columnar form). As well as tree specimens, extra larch were added to ensure that dappled shade would follow on for future generations and improve the age distribution of the larch. Hazel was added for wildlife and to provide cover and shelter at lower layers.

Along a separate deviating path, quite a few evergreens were planted to give the feel of seclusion from the road, among them Serbian spruce, Portugese laurel and bay.

Years later, a new path was created closer to the north/south boundary of the Arboretum, which now forms part of the main circuitous route, and has since been paved with hoggin because of the extent of foot traffic. This additional path allows greater accessibility into this wonderful and intricate space, ensuring visitors can get close to many of the specimens to examine them in detail.

# Stumpery

The most eclectic part of the Stumpery has to be the famous 'Wall of Gifts'. His Royal Highness is fortunate enough to receive many gifts from all over the world, which he is proud to display at Highgrove. Several such gifts are featured in the specifically created Wall of Gifts – these are stone gifts, mostly students' work, which The Prince has given a happy home. Here the presents are arranged in a cohesive way to form a brilliant and fascinating sculpture. The wall sits centre stage in a quiet clearing, offset with just a simple carpet of bulbs and woodland plants which contrast with its clearly defined architectural angles.

This was an ingenious idea, suggested by the Bannermans, devised to accommodate some of The Prince's gifts as well as samples of work by masonry apprentices. Fred Ind constructed the wall and cleverly managed to build it in such a way as to look uncontrived, with all of the individual artefacts carefully placed in a random, haphazard way.

Although the structure is a huge highlight in the Stumpery, the effervescent planting holds its own too, complementing the green oak artefacts and carefully planned to hold the interest for much of the growing season. The palette is kept simple with pale creams, greens and white, which add to the calm, charismatic feel of this highly individual area.

The flowers of the tall, demure martagon lilies are fading at the beginning of August, but their seedheads are left intact as they create valuable silhouettes standing proud above the lower plantings. The hydrangeas work particularly well in this sheltered space, adding subtle but welcome colour now and blending well with the

BELOW The Wall of Gifts is a stunning collection of pieces given to The Prince, constructed by Fred Ind and Paul Duckett.

foliage of the hostas, ferns and hellebores among the open woodland. The less well-known *Hydrangea heteromalla*, with its white flowers and quirky peeling bark is grown here, along with groups of the better known oak-leaved hydrangea (*H. quercifolia*) and *Hydrangea aspera*, with its flat heads of murky violet flowers set among bold velvety leaves.

The Sail Gate, so-called because it has an unusual sloping top rail that looks like a sail, leads out from the Stumpery towards the Lower Orchard. It was designed by Willie Bertram in 1991. The wall adjacent to the gate consists of motifs, such as The Prince of Wales feathers, and will soon have a new arch, which is being designed by students from the City and Guilds School of Design.

BELOW Tree ferns, ferns, hostas and hydrangeas sumptuously cover every inch of ground in the Stumpery with contrasting greens.

RIGHT A two-metre high replica of the Isis (based on the Egyptian Ibis), surveys the tiny Japanese Moss Garden.

# Stumpery Moss Garden

In wet Summers, the tiny moss garden, which occupies a space of just a few square metres in the Stumpery, appears to be made of lush, emerald velvet. Prince Charles had coveted a moss garden for many years, and in 2003 began having discussions in earnest about the possibility of creating one. Then, in 2011, the Kyoto Moss Garden was created as a gift from Iue International and the Highgrove Florilegium Japan Team, designed by the House of Sen. It was created by fifth-generation gardeners of the House of Sen, the Takemura brothers.

This extraordinary garden is full of intricate detail and meaning, the idea being that when someone enters this small Japanese oasis, it should feel evocative and, most importantly, should represent whatever the person entering it feels and imagines.

The focus of the garden is a low, mossy mound that portrays the mountains, and the path that encircles it represents boulders rising along a coast. The sculpture of a bird stands at the back edge of the moss lawn; it is a two-metre replica of the sculpture Isis in Hyde Park, which was created by sculptor Simon Gudgeon based on the Egyptian ibis, and was given to The Prince as a gift.

The garden is framed by a cluster of striking, single pink camellias that have been grown together to create a sensational and unusual hedge. Eventually they will be replaced with plants originating from cuttings from an ancient camellia, which was grown from a 600-year-old seed found in the soil of an eleventh-century temple in Kyoto. The hedge provides a beautiful aesthetic detail, but it also has a symbolic purpose, in representing the division between man and the natural world.

The construction of this garden was carefully devised by Debs Goodenough, following discussions with a moss expert from Edinburgh Botanic Gardens. Many mosses prefer acid soils and the soil in the Stumpery is neutral. It was decided to plant several types of mosses so those that tolerate more alkaline conditions will thrive and take over, and the others will die out. The ground had to be carefully

prepared so that the mosses would establish. First the grass was weeded out and then the area was recontoured according to the design. A plastic sheet was spread over this mound, which was topped with capillary matting and a thin layer of fine, sieved Highgrove compost firmed over it to provide a moist but well-drained soil. Debs collected mosses from the Birkhall Estate and from around the grounds at Highgrove and, working with the designers, carefully planted the clumps of moss then covered the plants with black netting to keep the blackbirds off. All in all, around six different types of moss were used, which were 'patchworked together' and watered in with rainwater. The number of different types has reduced naturally over the years, with two becoming vastly dominant.

The following Summer was extremely dry, and the moss suffered, turning rather brown, but fortunately this is not too alarming, because moss does have a tendency to go into dormancy in droughts, but it invariably recovers when the rains start. The beautifully textured mound is carefully tended throughout the year so it always looks inviting and any stray weeds are removed by hand. The lush, springy surface looks healthy in Summer but it is really at its best during the Winter months when the moss is deliciously velvety and green.

RIGHT A glimpse of the Orchard can be seen through the Moorish doorway.

OVERLEAF The Carpet Garden is much like stepping into another world. The yellow *Brugmansia* 'Angel's Trumpet' is the main contender here, flowering in six-week cycles.

# Carpet Garden

The planting in the Carpet Garden becomes heavy with scent and strong colours in late Summer. Beautiful intense purple violas, *Viola* 'Martin', which flower from April to October and have a deep, vibrant violet-blue flower, fill several terracotta pots. The rectangular beds are picked out in dwarf hedges of *Berberis thunbergii* f. *atropurpurea* 'Atropurpurea Nana' which have intense dark purple foliage that frames the plantings. There are pink roses, too, such as *Rosa* Bonica, *Rosa gallica* var. *officinalis* (native to Turkey) and *R.* 'Duchesse de Montebello', which add fragrance that hangs in the air, cleverly confined to the space by the high surrounding walls.

Elsewhere, magenta pelargoniums, white geraniums (*Geranium clarkei* 'Kashmir White'), *Iris sibirica* in a striking mauve (flowering in June) and a variety of lilies in complementary shades add to the pattern of this amazing carpet. Old gnarled standard vines, figs and standard *Citrus × Microcarpa* (a hybrid of a tangerine and kumquat and one of the hardiest of the citrus) reach higher than the carpet fillers, standing sentry around the edges of the design and transporting you a long way from Gloucestershire, across to the Mediterranean.

Around the edges are other tantalizing plants, which create a rich, continental atmosphere, such as *Hydrangea macrophylla* 'Merveille Sanguine' whose intensely coloured mopheads burst out of pots by the door. These stunning hydrangeas, which are of a rich plum red fading to magenta, are sumptuous plants. Originally a myrtle hedge was grown here, but it did not thrive and so has since been replaced by box hedging. Much of the planting is mulched and shown off against pinky chippings which tone with the orange tiles that are used throughout. Olive trees in pots add another Mediterranean touch and adorn the raised platform that leads from the Orchard entrance.

This hidden, secret garden has been laid out according to a favourite Turkish carpet of Prince Charles's. It has a traditional *chahar-bagh*, or four-fold design, and at the heart of the garden (or carpet) there is a raised fountain which sits in the centre of a Moroccan-inspired, scalloped, marble bowl. The low bubbling fountain and the sound of the gently moving water adds to the calm and authenticity of this Islamic garden. This white marble bowl rests on a beautifully mosaic-tiled octagonal plinth which is surrounded by another, larger, raised, mosaic tiled octagon. The hard landscaping of these octagons is softened by four symmetrically arranged beds which surround them and rills of water which run through the planting within them, adding extra sparkle, interest and lustre.

Originally there was just one canopy shaped in a Moorish arch (also called the Keyhole Arch and the Horseshoe Arch) which stood over the central entrance on one of the short sides, but His Royal Highness has now added another at the far end of the garden, under which a seat could be added. Elsewhere, splendid decorated wooden doors painted with bold Saudi Arabian designs and a ceramic plate with Arabic calligraphy add authenticity and texture.

Chelsea show gardens are created to be dramatic and shine for six days, but this garden has been developed so that it now gives pleasure for many months of the year. Clever alterations to the planting now extend their seasons of interest, several tender plants have also been replaced by more hardy specimens (the pomegranate trees sadly failed to thrive and the *Tamarix* just got too big), and alterations have been made to the layout to accommodate more people in the space – for instance, the viewing platform has been elevated so you can view the 'carpet' from above and the paths were widened.

The addition of this Carpet Garden offers a totally different dimension to the overall scheme at Highgrove. It impresses the point that the gardens here are eclectic – their creator is much travelled, has diverse and far-ranging interests as well as a real passion for gardens and gardening. Bringing his Chelsea garden to Highgrove means many more people can enjoy this exciting piece of paradise and watch its development and growth.

# Parkland

The beautiful Parkland that surrounds the house was one of the factors which persuaded His Royal Highness that this was the property for him. The magnificent ancient trees set in pasture form a beautiful setting for the house and gardens, providing spectacular views from many points. In early morning these old trees throw long shadows across the dewy grass, while during the heat of the day cattle can be seen clustered around the squat, dark shadows next to the ancient gnarled trunks.

In August the lush Spring leaves of these Parkland trees have usually turned a deep green and look sensational against the often brilliant-blue Summer sky. The spreading canopies, having been browsed for hundreds of years by cattle and sheep, have flat undersides and provide shade to help shelter The Prince's livestock from the strong sun and flies. Often you can see sleek, beautiful cattle grazing the grass; even the herd adds colour, including the breeds Aberdeen Angus, black, stocky beef cattle, and the more delicate brown and white Ayrshires, a Scottish dairy breed with attractive orange or brown markings.

In the smallest field, known as the Horse Paddock, you may well see four magnificent bulls, heads down pulling on the grass. During wetter Summers, and mainly in July or August, there may be a flush of fresh, light green growth on the trees, known as Lammas growth (Lammas Day is a Celtic festival that falls on 1 August). However, Lammas growth generally declines with the age of the tree, so the old oaks and ash show fewer signs of these Summer shoots than the younger trees.

The wood pastures, or Parkland, is divided into separate fields – Tanners Park, Middle Park or Horse Paddock – which means the grazing can be more productive because the livestock can be rotated between them, which allows the resting fields to recover. Some of these fields are divided with hedges, planted by His Royal Highness himself, and some with walls. This landscape has a quintessential parkland feel due to the informal planting of many specimen trees within the grassland.

These trees are set at spacings of 40 metres or so and include massive oaks, both *Quercus robur* (English oak) and the Lucombe oak (*Quercus × hispanica* 'Lucombeana'), which is a cross between *Querus cerris* and *Q. suber* (the cork oak), and is unusual in that it retains its leaves over Winter. There is the occasional sweet chestnut too, with its characteristic deeply furrowed bark. These furrows run along the trunk longitudinally but are apt to spiral or twist around it as it ages, providing a wonderful textured look to the tree.

When The Prince first came to Highgrove, there was a massive ancient ash tree in Middle Park and John White, who was advising The Prince on planting trees and their care, became concerned because it was looking extremely sick. The only course of action he could recommend was to pollard it – to cut the old limbs back to the main trunk. The long unhealthy branches weigh down the tree and so in a high wind, it would be more likely to fall. Although ash trees are frequently pollarded, there were no records stating what happened if a tree of over three hundred years old were pruned so severely. The Prince's response to this extreme suggestion was, 'I will brace myself for the shock of seeing the poor old tree looking as though it has been to the barber'. The extreme treatment was recorded in the *Corporation of London Tree Pollarding* book. Thankfully, the tree survived and responded well to its surgery.

LEFT The sheep nibble fine grasses while the cattle prefer longer, coarser vegetation.

RIGHT Some trees in the wood pastures around Highgrove have been dated at 1680.

Highgrove has many interesting 'firsts' in all aspects of horticulture and arboriculture. The Prince is willing to experiment and develop new ideas and techniques and does so thoughtfully with the back up and advice from specialists in the relevant areas. As a result, the Parkland now has a diverse collection of trees of various ages, and this diversity is boosted as The Prince plants more young trees. Most of the new trees are native oaks that will eventually form magnificent pasture or parkland trees. They work beautifully within this landscape, complementing its quintessentially British feel, and in addition they support a vast amount of wildlife. The oaks are planted as small specimens, usually under a metre tall, as they establish fast and grow into a far better specimen than those planted at a larger size, promising to be an enduring part of this Parkland for many future generations.

Purple carrot
*Daucus carota*

# SEPTEMBER

'Now is the time the sheep go back on the Meadow to maintain the unchanging management regime of a wildflower meadow. I never underestimate the value of the 'golden hoof' in the great scheme of biodiversity and now I hope I have found the answer to the problem of sheep eating and damaging the bark of trees that I have planted in the Meadow: by grazing Shropshire sheep, a breed that is reputed not to eat trees. We shall see … September used to be the month when colder, frostier nights would herald clearer, fresher days, but advancing climate change is rapidly altering our more equable and predictable climate.'

# Kitchen Garden

AS SUMMER BEGINS TO WANE AND THE landscape softens its hues, the growth and pace of the garden settles back into a more leisurely pace. The grazing sheep in the Meadow bring this stunning landscape to life and the Kitchen Garden is fuller than ever, as the huge tunnels drip with bountiful stems of sweet peas and beans, courgettes and squash burgeon and ripen in the last rays of Summer. Sitting on the Terrace Garden is an equally dramatic sensory experience in September; here you are surrounded by clusters of pots overflowing with lush foliage and vivid colours. Colour levels in the Cottage Garden have ramped up too – they look even stronger, less bleached with the lower angle of the less intense sun. There is a 'gentle urgency' in the air, to make the most of these days, harvesting and gathering and preparing for the Winter ahead.

In September, the Kitchen Garden is teeming with an abundance of fruit and vegetables that have ripened; flourishing courgettes are swallowing the ground and the turnover of yellow flowers to mini marrows is fast and frequent – catching them all when they are midgets to keep the production line running takes vigilance. The onions have grown and are now gently eased from the ground to dry off in the sun before the dew softens them and lets in rot. The best will be stored inside for overwinter use.

It is fascinating to examine the burgeoning beds at the end of the day, looking at the crops drinking in the evening sunlight, to see what has grown superbly and what hasn't. Every year varies, with its new successes and new failures, and doubtless this Kitchen Garden has taught scores of gardeners a thing or two over the many, disparate years.

LEFT *Actaea racemosa* 'Atropurpurea', or black cohosh, mingles with pink Japanese anemones.

BELOW In the foreground, *Sedum* (Herbstfreude Group) tones in well with *Echinacea purpurea* 'Bressingham Hybrids' behind.

OVERLEAF The apple tunnel is swathed in ripening fruit at this time of year.

ABOVE Evergreen hedges of
*Teucrium × lucidrys* replaced the box
hedges when box blight took hold.
These hedges are clipped after
flowering as the bees love the nectar.

RIGHT In September, rosy red,
organic apples ('Discovery') are ready
to be picked for the table, shop,
store or kitchen.

Gardeners often despair about the drabness of late
Summer but the Kitchen Garden is as full of interest
now as it was in Spring. One of the crowning glories is
the centrepiece, the circle of crab apples, *Malus* 'Golden
Hornet', which surround the central pool. As Autumn
creeps in, these trees are covered with a mass of deep,
golden-yellow, conspicuous crab apples that adorn the tree
for many weeks, contrasting with the deep green leaves.
Later on the leaves turn butter yellow before falling. These
trees are highly decorative as well as valuable: backlit by
the low Autumnal sun they glow with halos like Christmas
baubles, but they also produce prolific amounts of pollen
from their lavish white flowers in Spring, which is highly
useful for pollinating other apple trees.

At The Prince's suggestion, the trees were planted and
trained with linked branches to create a crown effect.
The training work is carried out in Autumn and the new
whippy growths from the Summer are pulled down and
tied in. Once completed they look wonderful and their
outline in Winter is much admired.

This is just one of many spectacular sights now. The
walls are hung with firm, golden pears, yellow and green
gages and ruby-coloured plums all highlighting the strong
lines of the trained branches that are anchored to the walls.
In 2003 some of the older, diseased trees were removed
and replaced. On the north wall a Morello cherry was
added, along with several espalier pears on the west and
south walls and four fig trees on the south side. One of
the old wall-trained pears was in need of rejuvenation so
it was cut down about a foot above ground level and the
new growth was then retrained. Because the plant was so
well established, it took far less time to form a well-filled-out
espalier than if it had been grubbed out and replaced.

By the entrance of the Kitchen Garden, the redcurrants
are artfully trained as rough fans on the north-facing
wall and do surprisingly well in this cool position (as do
gooseberries).

The herb garden is focused in the circular beds around
the pool and it still looks trim and productive at this time.
The original collection of herbs was a gift from the Sussex

branch of the Women's Institute. These beds were renovated in 2010 because the horseradish had taken over, but it has now been restricted to a pot. The supremely fragrant and versatile lemon verbena, *Aloysia citrodora* (superb as a hot infusion) is also grown in pots due to its slightly tender nature, as is lemon grass, so it can easily be moved under cover when frost threatens.

The art of producing succulent, fresh, flavoursome herbs is to keep picking to prevent them becoming tired and leggy, so the royal chefs use them freely for salads, sauces and seasoning. More than 30 different herbs are grown here in addition to the regular staples (such as rosemary, sage and thyme); having such an extensive range gives great scope for the chefs to exercise their creativity.

The borders have highlights now too. *Gladiolus* 'Green Star' looks fresh and a perfect green among the other more autumnal hues. This plant does not fade to yellow as other green gladioli do but stays true. *Eucomis bicolor*, the pineapple lily, with its pale green star-shaped flowers is another fresh-faced addition too; it tones well with the light lime green of *Philadelphus coronarius* 'Aureus'. The blue asters, ruby sedums and pink anemones bring more colour with swatches of favourites from the royal palette.

One of the most pleasant views of the garden is from and through the foliage-fringed arbour that sits against the south wall, with views focused down the mixed border. This charming, unassuming building is made from oak, and describes a semi-circle on plan. It has gentle curving beams, elegant timber pillars and is draped with sweet-smelling honeysuckle and the fived-leaved akebia, *Akebia quinata* 'Alba'. This semi-evergreen, vigorous climber has creamy white flowers in Spring which transform into oddly shaped, chocolate-purple fruits later in the year.

LEFT The rose arbours look romantically wild at the end of the Summer and it isn't until February that they are tamed.

ABOVE The moss on the Italian fountain increases steadily over the years as no protective cover is used in the Winter. This only adds to the Kitchen Garden's enchanting feel.

RIGHT This water lily was given to The Prince as a gift and helps shade the water in order to reduce the algal bloom.

The 'golden hooves' of the sheep help tread the wild flower seeds, aiding their establishment.

## Meadow

At this time of year, after the Meadow has been cut, the grass is usually tired and yellow, and it takes a few weeks for it to darken and burst into life again. The new grass looks quite thin to start with, so September is the time to sow any particularly sparse areas with extra seed or add plug plants to boost the flower power in the Meadows. Every year the balance of the flowers at Highgrove changes; what were star performers one year may become runners-up another. This dynamic change through the seasons and years is what makes meadow gardening exciting.

Gardeners are now making a real difference in helping to compensate for the dramatic loss of wildlife in the countryside. Environmental enthusiasts such as Prince Charles have illustrated what effects can be achieved by letting some of the garden grow a little wild, and now other gardeners are switching to a more environmentally friendly approach too.

Some gardeners have tried to create meadows in their gardens and can easily become disenchanted. Debs Goodenough advises frustrated gardeners on a range of scales from micro, metre-square patches, to rolling acres. If you are tentative about creating a wilder area, Debs advocates starting on a mini scale, 'This may just be a few square metres. Seed is expensive, so just see how you like it and concentrate your energies on a small, intensive patch. Watch it and enjoy seeing how it progresses, collect seed from it and re-use the seed to increase its impact and size.'

This time of year, from September into October, is the ideal time to create a new patch, with grass cut extremely closely, then scarified or raked well – preferably before rain. At Highgrove, the seed mix used is carefully chosen to suit the conditions, just as it should be in any garden. Debs advises that if the grass sward is quite close and is vigorous, the best mixture includes yellow rattle, which will inhibit the growth of the grass.

Early Autumn is also the best time to put in any plug plants, so they can establish well over Winter before any potential droughts in Spring. Debs also advocates planting wild daffodils, *Narcissus pseudonarcissus,* now in random patterns to 'get the meadow through the shaggy period in March and April', and the subtle attributes of this native daffodil complement the wilder look.

# Terrace Garden

Now is the time when the Autumn days start to draw in and the frenetic Summer's growth begins to slow. The low Autumn light has a magic about it too – the colours are stronger, less flat, and the flowers and foliage also appear to have more texture and depth to them. This is one of the best times of year to enjoy an al fresco drink or meal here, surrounded by the scents from the highly aromatic rosemary, lavender and sage bushes that form comfortably shaped pillows of neat foliage. The apricot flowers of *Rosa* 'Jude the Obscure' lend their scent to the air as do those of the highly fragrant, coral pink floribunda rose, *Rosa* 'L'Aimant'. The olive trees with their now thick canopy of grey-green leaves soak up the late Summer sun with relish.

The Terrace Garden shows itself off well – the pots are bursting with colour as the occupants have been fed, watered and regularly scrutinised by a regal eye. The drama and colour of the pots contrasts with the yellowing of the leaves of the strident pleached hornbeams that form the outer frame beyond the golden yews that line the Thyme Walk.

The design of the terrace and pool was a collaboration between Lady Salisbury and Prince Charles. A key function of this prime space is to have an area of hard landscaping so that chairs can be set out in the warmer months. The design process went underway in 1984, with the architect David Blissett's help.

The octagonal pool is a massive draw for wildlife, pulling them in close to the house windows so they can be regularly watched and observed. The water is designed to be low key, simple and restful rather than a showstopper to distract from the view.

The design of the millstone feature was a collaboration between the sculptor William Pye and The Prince. The pebbles in the base of the pool have been collected by The Prince on his many travels and are subtly different, representing a fascinatingly wide geological range of rocks. Frequently propped against the inside of the pool is a woven willow ramp (made at Highgrove from home-grown willow) which is around 60 centimetres long and allows newts, young frogs and other creatures to access the vertical sides of the pool.

For some time after the pool was complete, Prince Charles was concerned about its water level: he was convinced there was a leak as the level was dropping too quickly. Then one day he spied the gardeners using it as a dunking pool to quickly water the pots. Mystery solved!

The choice of material for the terrace paving was originally intended to consist of pebbles from Chesil Beach in Dorset. In the 1980s, natural materials such as these were sometimes collected and moved. However, there was a change of heart and The Prince made the decision to use Pennant stone, a durable sandstone (often used for paving and roofing) that comes relatively locally from the Bristol/south Wales area. This has been laid in an irregular chequerboard pattern with squares of entire paving stones interspersed with squares of thin bands of the stone laid edge-on, which has been employed in many areas for centuries, and here it creates a charming, disorganised surface. There are then three bands of small, square stone setts laid around the edge of the pool as a coping, and four large terracotta pots outline the edge of the pool, to ensure that only birds and small creatures pop in and out.

The paving looks less formal by virtue of the irregular chequerboard pattern, but it is made even softer by the numerous plants that creep, grow and thrive here. Throughout the year a succession of plants make their appearance.

BELOW *Acidanthera bicolor* 'Murielae', the Abyssinian gladiolus, is a half-hardy bulb that needs to be overwintered in frost-free conditions.

RIGHT The splendid Acidantheras are planted in the wigwams so that they are bursting out at eye-level. This area of hard landscaping contrasts with the soft trickle of the octagonal pool.

In February, after the snow-white snowdrops start to fade, there are masses of purple crocuses poking through, transforming the hard grey paving lines into a growing linear pattern of brilliant purple. Primroses are punctuating the cracks and joints in April and *Alchemilla mollis* billows forth in May, coming back later for a repeat performance following a quick cut back from the gardening team. Chamomile and oregano feature too, as fragrant additions that release their delicate scents when crushed underfoot. Many gardeners like plants in paving, but on the west Terrace it almost seems there is paving among the plants.

The pots on the Terrace are an important element of the design; they offer a wonderful opportunity to try new plants and create a variety of effects, and as such the arrangements are rarely the same two years in succession. Some years tubs of tulips are plunged into the pots in April, when the skimmia and topiarised box plants are removed, having made a good display through the Winter. After the tulips, huge, thirsty daturas or brugmansias, with their extraordinary trumpet-like flowers, might be planted out. These are more commonly known as 'angel's trumpets' because of their huge, pendulous, trumpet flowers which are produced in regular cycles through the Summer, and can apparently give you hallucinogenic dreams if you fall asleep under them! Fine, carefully selected pelargoniums come out from greenhouses in May after the frosts are passed, and are strong favourites here too. 'Rembrandt', the beautiful Regal pelargonium with a lighter mauve edge around a darker purple centre, and 'Marchioness of Bute', a beauty that is almost black but edged with purple, are regular contenders for these prime positions.

Other plants on the Terrace have been chosen to provide scent, good year-round colour and just because they are favourites. The small, square beds that sit at the base of the olives are filled with Mediterranean-type plants that spill over the paving, hiding any hint of a straight line. *Salvia officinalis* 'Purpurascens', the dusky, purple-leaved sage, and *Helichrysum italicum*, the curry plant, are repeated to fill these important places, toning well with the feel and colour provided by the olives' leaves.

The new Summerhouse
is a place for The Prince to work
without having to curtail his
writing during showers.

# Cottage Garden

This is no ordinary Cottage Garden where many plants
achieve their pinnacle of colour in the earlier months of
Summer. This space looks especially magical now, in early
Autumn, as the soft light levels enhance the delights of
the later flowers on the many perennials and annuals
which are cleverly planted to enchant the visitors.

The Indian bean tree, *Catalpa bignonioides* 'Aurea',
which was given to Prince Charles for his fiftieth birthday
by Sir Elton John, often bears pods at this time of year.
It has become an increasingly popular tree, as it is easy,
fast-growing and has resplendent white flowers in such
mammoth clusters that they can obscure the leaves
altogether around July. Curiously, it does not come from
India, nor produce real beans; it was in fact first recorded
in America, and the botanist who discovered it first saw
it growing in the field of a Native American tribe, hence
the name. The pods do look like beans and can grow to
well over a foot long and its heart-shaped leaves fall with
no dramatic colour change after the first frosts.

Apart from the colourful buttress borders, which are
brimming with well-orchestrated colour, other strong
performers are now coming into play. Many phlox,
including *Phlox paniculata* 'Bright Eyes' is one such.
This produces a good second flush of flowers after its
earlier display due to the dead heading and feeding it has
received since then. The cone flower *Echinacea purpurea*
Bressingham hybrids is still producing its bright, rosy-
purple flowers with distinctive orange-brown, button-like
centres, while the pinky-burgundy flowers of *Sedum* 'Vera
Jameson' tone beautifully with its blue-grey foliage. The
bewitching panicles of red/purple small, tubular, fragrant
flowers of *Buddleja davidii* 'Dartmoor' pull in the hungry
butterflies who enjoy the warmer microclimate of this
protected area. *Cornus kousa* var. *chinensis* has usually lost
its strawberry-like, fleshy red fruit by now, but it retains
interest as it starts to produce deep crimson Autumn
colour as the days become chillier. The *Cotinus coggygria*
'Notcutt's variety' also looks impressive; the panicles of
flowers slowly change colour and are often a dusky pink
at this time, which looks like a haze of smoke around
and above the leaves.

The structural planting counterbalances the fiery Autumn tones with solid greens, creating a striking site. The Irish junipers near the circular stone seat create strong vertical accents among the planting, as do the Irish yews elsewhere in this part of the garden. A seldom-used evergreen growing here is *Ligustrum japonicum* 'Rotundifolium', a grafted form with small, glossy, almost camellia-like leaves, making it compact and quite architectural.

The new Summerhouse has proved a great success, offering welcome shelter from the variable late Summer showers. Two stag-headed oaks were removed from the estate into a cart shed where they were carved up by the estate team of Fred Ind, Steve Staines and Paul Duckett, who then created this structure, and only finished when the gardens were opened in March 2013. The delay was due to it being the coldest Spring on record. Many things that were expected to be in full flower still had yet to appear. 'I do hope the visitors are not disappointed,' Prince Charles had worried while briefing his guides on the changes that had occurred during the Winter. The visitors might well have been chillier than usual, but many repeat visitors thought it looked better than ever.

The design for the rustic Summerhouse building was a collaboration between Prince Charles and Mark Hoare. Mark was a student at The Prince's Institute of Architecture (formerly The Prince's Foundation for the Building Community) which is a charity that aims to teach traditional design and architecture so as to put the relevant people and communities at the centre of the design process.

The roof of oak shingles is gently undulating, as though time has caused it to settle in gracefully. The massive trunks that support the roof sit on coursed rubble stone and the finial, a carved-oak acorn, sits atop the roof; another carved panel is set into the rear wall. The whole structure is low and compact, so as to reinforce the Cottage Garden feel.

At this time of year the building comes into its own and Prince Charles often works outside in this sheltered space. Previously in showery Summers, cushions, chairs, table and paperwork had to be endlessly carted in and out of the house but this rustic structure, tucked snugly in among a wide border of scented plants, now affords shelter when required.

ABOVE A generous clump of the magnificently easy plume poppy, *Macleaya macrocarpa* 'Kelways Coral Plume' is in the foreground and frames the view of the Indian Gate.

RIGHT Two supreme annuals, *Nicotiana langsdorffii* 'Lemon Tree', intertwined with the unusual but striking *Cuphea viscosissima*.

ABOVE RIGHT Repeated clusters of *Hebe rakaiensis* guard the corners of the Cottage Garden pathway, with more ephemeral planting behind.

FAR RIGHT *Aster frikartii* 'Wunder von Stäfa', the long-flowering aster with excellent mildew resistance, together with *Nicotiana alata* 'Whisper Mix' and *Cuphea*.

*Pyrus communis*
'Beurré Hardy'

# OCTOBER

'October is a time of harvest in the Kitchen Garden and in the apple orchards. Hopefully, there will be some pears – juicy ones, if we are lucky, and not ones made of cotton wool or blotting paper. The eagerly anticipated first Brussels sprout of the season heralds a Winter diet of this delectable vegetable, as well as carrots, leeks, cabbages and potatoes. This is the month to give thanks for the eternal partnership between Man and Nature and to remember that unless we give back to Nature in equal measure to what we take from her, she will no longer be able to sustain us into the future. It is a subtle and reverential balance that has to be struck, but has been all too readily forgotten in the rush to exploit.'

THERE IS A SENSE THAT THE GARDEN IS slowing down now. The Lawns and Meadows that encircle the house have gone green once more and have a restful air about them. The plants that make up the Thyme Walk have fully bonded after a Summer of growth and woven themselves into a tight and flowing carpet. As one season moves into another, the golden Autumn colours across the gardens are truly spectacular, but it is most impressive in the Arboretum where the Japanese maples and Sargent's cherry (*Prunus sargentii*) lend their fiery colours to the scene. A sense of tranquillity pervades the air in the Stumpery, the lush greens of the many hostas and ferns adding a serene and peaceful atmosphere to this otherwise wild garden. The Summer weather may be waning, but the show still goes on.

ABOVE Autumnal tints are highlighted by the shiny red fruits of this crab apple, *Malus* 'Evereste'.

LEFT This Japanese maple is one of many unusual varieties planted in the Arboretum over the last 30 years.

RIGHT A *Pyracantha* (firethorn), which has bitter, red berries beloved by birds, is trained on the wall in the Terrace Garden.

# Thyme Walk

The golden yews that punctuate this garden have once again turned golden yellow with their fluff of Summer growth, although this will shortly be transformed back to a strong green when their striking forms receive their annual clip. Above them the pleached hornbeams echo the golden tints of the yews, their lines of foliage marking out the shape of this enticing walkway with long tracts of corrugated bright yellow and ochre leaves, which pull your eye beyond to the Lime Avenue. The red-twigged limes (*Tilia platyphyllos* 'Rubra') that make up this garden have turned a yellow-green and their long shoots often wave in the gentle Autumn breeze.

In the light fog of October, the thyme plants look particularly picturesque. They are no longer the haze of purples, pinks and reds as they were when in full flower, but their undulating mounds of foliage created by mixing the various forms of thyme plants is striking.

When the plants have finished flowering they are immediately cut back or sheared over. This has the effect of rejuvenating the plants so that by now, in October, they have a lush, healthy and buxom look. Caring for this expansive stretch of different thymes can be challenging; most particularly keeping the rabbits away. Rabbits and pheasants will do a great deal of damage to thymes, so if you live in the country, temporary fencing or netting laid over them until they get established will help.

When the Thyme Walk was initially planted, the heavy soil that sits on the underlying clay was lightened with the addition of sand and gravel. But over the years, the level sank a little, presumably due to the foot traffic. Another complication is that the lawns either side are deliberately cultivated as 'mown green spaces', burgeoning with free-seeding herbs as well as seeding grasses, which also tend to infiltrate the Thyme Walk. When these lawn weeds and grasses are in the 'Lawn' areas they are beautiful, but once they spread into the thyme they become irritating weeds.

The thyme plants were supplied by Jekka McVicar, who ran an herb nursery near Bristol at the time. One memorable day in 2001, Jekka drove up with 4,000 thyme plants of 15 different varieties. These included the prostrate types, such as *Thymus serpyllum*, the upright forms such as *T.* 'Fragrantissimus' (the orange-scented thyme) and the mounding, or slightly raised thymes such as *T. pulegioides* 'Bertram Anderson'. These latter types are short enough to walk on, as are the creeping forms, whereas the uprights tend to be walked around. The thymes were then planted in groups of six to nine of the same variety together.

Once the plants are actively growing, a light grazing, as with grass, is usually quite beneficial. Apart from the annual trimming with shears, replacement plants do need to go in on a two- to six-year cycle, depending on the type of thyme used and the drainage. Cuttings are taken in July and will root in a few weeks, and then can be potted and ready to plant the following Autumn or Spring.

When Debs Goodenough became Head Gardener in 2008, a lot of thymes were dying, which was caused by the Mypex (a weed-suppressing mat), impeding the drainage. Debs had the difficult job of removing sections of this and cleaning the soil, before replanting all the plants.

The hard work was worth it, though, because sitting among the thymes and enjoying their scent and views across the gardens, observing the changing colours in the crisp Autumn air, is a restful way to pass the time.

The Thyme Walk is 95 metres long, so fabulously huge in scale. Unfortunately, lawn weeds and grasses continually self-seed into it.

# Stumpery

In many of Highgrove's gardens at this time of year, the most dramatic change comes from the turning of the foliage – and this is most evident in the Stumpery. Here the range of carefully selected acers, amelanchiers and the katsura tree, *Cercidiphyllum magnificum* put on a show-stopping display of colour. The latter is a smaller form of *C. japonicum*, but it too has excellent Autumn colour, with the foliage turning a rich yellow interwoven with peachy highlights, and its fallen leaves scent the air with an aroma like burnt toffee.

The Stumpery, with its iconic buildings, dramatic planting and calm atmosphere has been a favourite haven of Prince Charles for many years. He had a memorial built here to the poet Ted Hughes, called 'The Temple of Worthies', which is set in a half circle and defined by a low mound overlaid with entwined stumps. The building itself

ABOVE The inscription on one of the temples reads the Shakespearean quote: *'Find tongues in trees, books in running brooks, sermons in stone and good in everything'.*

RIGHT The two beautifully detailed temples face each other across a grassy glade.

is made of green oak, a large amount of which is textured or worked in a fashion called 'vermiculation' (to give a worm-eaten appearance). This type of dressing is more commonly associated with stone, but when applied to green oak it looks magnificent and ties in with the rustic feel of its surroundings. Four large acorns sit on the top above a central pyramid, and around the base are three benches, also made of vermiculated green oak.

Prince Charles was extremely fond of his grandmother, and when she died in 2002, he decided to dedicate the memorial to her, moving the bronze plaque dedicated to Ted Hughes to one of the temples. A relief of the Queen Mother was added in which she is wearing her favourite gardening hat; she was a keen gardener and a huge influence on The Prince. At Birkhall (formerly her home,

which Prince Charles inherited), he is respectful of her input and has kept much of her original garden unchanged, with the enhancement of hedges and topiary.

The memorial to the Queen Mother complements the two temples; all three structures are bold and made of green oak, and these strong elements are woven together by the flowing mounds of the planted banks. A sea of hostas, ferns and other lower-growing plants flow freely, punctuated with the occasional orange-red of amelanchiers and Japanese maples.

Between the two temples and under the old oak tree is an outstanding sculpture, 'Goddess of the Woods: Spirit of Calm and Stillness', by the famous British sculptor David Wynne. This statue was commissioned for the original Woodland Garden in 1991 by The Prince. She is

made of Rosso Orbico marble and is extremely tactile –
you can feel her vertebrae as you run your fingers
down her back.

Various finishing touches and embellishments were
added to the temples later: two extremely fine carved oak
seats, complete with The Prince of Wales Feathers, were
designed by the Bannermans. Not only do they provide
an elegant resting place in each of the two temples for
visitors, but on one of them a leprechaun lounges, given
to The Prince by an Irish friend and called '*Fear Darrig*,' which
means 'Red Man'. The friend wrote, 'If the wee man with
the red beard makes an appearance in the garden, you
can rub his left cheek for luck and tell him what we
think of him.'

LEFT 'The Temple of Worthies'
is a memorial dedicated to the
Queen Mother and is made from
green oak, distressed to appear
vermiculated.

ABOVE RIGHT The Goddess of the
Woods statue, made of Rosso Orbico
marble, sits between the two temples
under an old oak.

RIGHT Tree ferns and mossy tree
stumps help create an other-worldly,
mystical atmosphere in the
Stumpery, unlike anything most
visitors have ever seen before.

# Arboretum

The Arboretum was designed to be outstanding in the Autumn – and it certainly is. Each year, as the specimen trees that have been successively planted from 1990 increase in girth and stature, so does the drama and the colour within this space. The sounds, smells and light of this open wooded plantation change dramatically with the seasons, becoming more peaceful now as everything slows down in preparation for the Winter.

There is no more frenetic growth from the trees and shrubs, and the grasses and herbs on the woodland floor begin to look sleepy in their Autumn dew. The woodland wildlife is becoming less visible as the days shorten, but the songs of blackbirds and thrushes still ring in the air. Bees can be heard too, busily working the ivy flowers, which have appeared in huge quantities on the older trees. These valuable flowers are crucial sources of nectar and pollen at this time of year, not just for the bees but for wasps, butterflies and flies too.

There are many acers in the full force of their stunning Autumn foliage now, and as they are in clumps of three or more specimens, they make a dramatic scene. *Acer palmatum* 'Osakazuki' runs to a strong scarlet, *A. japonicum* 'Aconitifolium' and *A. sieboldianum* light up with burnt orange and flame-red tints, while the deeply cut leaves of *A. japonicum* 'Vitifolium', which are spangled all over its bushy habit, change from apple green to rich cherry red. The specimens of Persian ironwood dotted through the

wood add personality with their eccentric, often multi-stemmed form and organic orange-coloured leaves.

There were many hazels planted here in the Nineties and these have largely been removed to make way for more exotic planting. As the Arboretum continues to develop, the understorey has changed from rough grass, dog's mercury and other natural vegetation to include more areas with bulbs and exotic shrubs to extend the range of plants and the colour levels.

October is a fabulous time to simply step back and admire the highlights of the garden, but it is also a busy time of year. During the Summer The Prince likes to start planning the next year's changes and developments; the garden at Highgrove is permanently undergoing 'tweaks'. Prince Charles has explained, 'I am always having new ideas about colour combinations, shapes and objects.' He will assess the performance of borders and plantings, or perhaps he may be inspired by a landscape he has enjoyed on his travels, works of art, or is motivated by a gift; he will then work out how best to place it, as if painting a series of pictures.

Any changes need to be put in place in the Autumn and Winter period, when the garden tours cease, so there is always planning underway in October and November. The decision may be made as to which trees, if any, should be felled, or thinned. If an area is overcrowded and low light

LEFT A close-up of *Acer palmatum* 'Osakazuki'. In this sheltered, shady spot, the dramatic colour lasts for several weeks.

ABOVE *Acer palmatum* 'Osakazuki', is one of the finest maples for spectacular Autumn colour.

levels are stunting the growth of the exotics closer to the ground, then the poorest, weakest trees will be selectively thinned. This ensures that the light levels do not dip too low when the existing tree canopies grow larger. Canopies of larger trees may be lifted now in order to increase light levels. Work will be carried out through the Winter months, when the foliage has fallen, to those trees that were earmarked that need attention.

Now is also the time when new bulbs will be planted and plans for additional shrubs will be finalised to ensure an even more beautiful and versatile display the following year.

Debs also keeps her eye on the ivy that is scrambling over the large trees. Ivy is generally thought to be a fairly positive addition to an arboretum; the flowers are rich for wildlife at a time of year when there is not much around in terms of nectar and pollen, and its shrubby nature as it matures makes a fabulous habitat for spiders, beetles, birds and even small mammals. However, it has been noticed that in high winds, ivy-clad trees tend to go first, due to the amount of weight it adds to the tree, which it is unable to sustain. So the policy is to keep watch, and when the ivy looks too dominant, it is removed.

The Prince's dedicated involvement for over 30 years right from the selection of his favourite trees and shrubs to overseeing the management of them is evident in this bit of utopia. Shaping the lower limbs of trees and shrubs is a task that he performs himself; anything that can be reached by his long-handled loppers is left so it can be shaped with his artist's eye.

BELOW The Prince selected trees for bursts of both Spring and Autumn colour. Japanese acers thrive here due to the deep forest marble soil and light shade.

OVERLEAF A central grassy ride leads to the Daughters of Odessa statue, partially surrounded by a bench of boulders (made of Welsh slate) and oak.

# The 'Lawn'

The Lawn, moist with early Autumn's light fog, is a serene space. Areas of grass in a garden are often thought of as 'breathing spaces', as they are uncomplicated, unifying areas that are simply treated, in contrast with the more structured parts of a garden.

There are some fine trees and pieces of topiary that are set out among the grass; the topiary will provide interest and structure throughout the Winter, but many of the deciduous trees are now preparing their foliage for their Autumn fall, their leaves turning into yellows, bronzes and reds, which stand out markedly in contrast to the dark hedging. Looking out from the house on an Autumn morning, you often see spiders' webs covered with dew hanging from the topiary.

Until December 2007 the dominant feature of the Lawn was the fine cedar of Lebanon, but sadly the reluctant decision was made to cut down the diseased tree. It had been attacked by a bracket fungus and then, as can happen, honey fungus set in. Spent mushroom compost was added in the belief that it contains *Trichoderma viride*, a fungus that will attack honey fungus.

A young cedar of Lebanon had been planted some way from the original in 1988 in anticipation of such a decision, and it is now growing well. These trees take far less time to reach their venerable plateaux; in about 75 years this young tree will have developed the look of a fine old specimen, hopefully something that the next few generations of the family will enjoy. A bronze sculpture of a design book of Leon Krier's (who designed Poundbury in Dorset) is under this tree, opened to display an intriguing housing layout. This was presented to His Royal Highness in 2001 when he opened a development in Germany.

Other trees have been planted in the Lawn over the years, including quite a number of topiary yews and some exotic specimens such as the tree of heaven (*Ailanthus altissima*) and the Chinese tulip tree (*Liriodendron chinense*). The Chinese tulip tree is far superior to the more common North American species, *Liriodendron tulipifera*. It is rare and threatened in the wild, but like the more familiar tulip tree, the foliage turns a beautiful butter-yellow now. More fine Autumn colour comes from the four groups of the Japanese flowering crab apple (*Malus floribunda*), which are now also showing off their small red and yellow fruits.

Several specimens of yew have been immaculately shaped to form a variety of fantastic structures, with no two designed identically, including a vast vase on a range of tiered plinths, a column and a back-to-back seat set into a geometrical piece of topiary. Not all of these are yet complete, some are work in progress, but they all become stronger statements as the garden matures.

There are five pieces of this topiary laid out in a loose quincunx (the shape of a five on a dice) on the ends of the Lawn nearest the house. They cast long shadows in the low Autumnal light, which accentuates their dramatic and varied forms. This end of the Lawn, nearer the house, is more formal than the other, which has more specimen trees with longer grass. At this time, though, the entire sward has had a fresh cut and new wildflower seeds will be germinating in the wilder patches, ready to surprise and delight next Summer.

The various shapes of topiary create long shadows in the Autumn sun. In its early years, the Lawn was used as a football pitch for the young Princes.

# Lower Orchard

In October the Orchard is flourishing with fruit: apples, pears, quinces and gages, to name but a few. It is a common sight to see Marion, who has been at Highgrove for 27 years, checking the ripeness of each fruit and packing large boxes, ready for the table, shop, store or kitchens, where they are bottled or juiced, or made into jam or chutney.

The apple store, which is kept at around 3°C, has its racks steadily filled over the next few months as the fruit ripens. Pears are one of His Royal Highness's favourite fruits, and many different varieties are grown at Highgrove – some are eaten fresh, and the others stored or bottled.

The Prince has added to the collection of pear trees over the years and many of the new ones planted in the orchard are varieties developed at the Delbard Nursery in France, whose breeding programme involves selecting for taste and disease resistance.

One hundred chickens were introduced to the Orchard in 2003, and now, as they have been so successful, their numbers are double that quantity. The chicken breeds have diversified; there are White Sussex, Marans (grey speckled) and some Buff Orpingtons too. The chickens not only add to the countryside appeal of the orchard,

BELOW The apples in the Lower Orchard are all completely organic.

ABOVE RIGHT Crab apples are excellent pollinators for apple trees; here, *Malus hupehensis* is laden with its cherry-like, small fruits.

but the eggs they lay are sold in the shop, local surrounding area and used in the vegetable box scheme. The chickens are also excellent at helping to keep the Orchard healthy, eating woolly aphids and many other pests that overwinter in the soil.

The Slovenian bee house, a present given to The Prince by the Slovenian government during a visit there, is an attractive and highly productive asset to the Orchard. The hives inside are positioned so the 'supers' are far easier to move and tend than in the more normal free-standing versions, and this arrangement also means honey can be harvested throughout the season, which is not possible with free-standing hives. With beekeeping on the increase, this type of bee house may well be less of a rarity in the near future.

Copper beech *Fagus sylvatica*
Japanese maple *Acer palmatum*

# NOVEMBER

'Nowadays it is usually late October or early November when the Autumn colours are at their best. My favourite place in the garden at this time is the Arboretum, where the stunning reds, yellows, golds and greens are lit up by the slanting sun. Having planted these acers so long ago with this aim in mind, it is wonderful when it works! When the leaves fall there is a momentary carpet of reds and yellows under the suddenly bare branches that forms another unforgettable moment in the cycle of the seasons.'

WALKING IN THE ARBORETUM WHEN the cool, early light catches the frost is magical. The trees discard their leaves quickly after the first cold descends and these freshly fallen leaves form a richly coloured and textured carpet that crackles underfoot. The Sanctuary seems somehow even more peaceful now, its ochre walls almost melting into the Autumn scene, and the Sundial Garden, previously overflowing with lavish, vibrant planting, has suddenly changed to a garden stripped to its fine structure. As Winter begins to settle in, the emphasis in Highgrove's garden is now on the dark topiary shapes, bare magnolias and the expansive views that have now become more visible through all of its carved openings.

BELOW The Victorian porch, added in 1893, is covered with *Vitis cognetiae*; its huge dinner plate-sized leaves colour best in poor soils.

RIGHT The toadstools, near the Stumpery, were a gift from a Yorkshire farmer. *Cyclamen hederifolium* adorn the base of this one.

# Arboretum

Although the visitors have now left Highgrove and the leaves have started floating to the ground, the Arboretum is still an eventful place in November. On a frosty morning the temperature is noticeably warmer here than elsewhere due to the canopies of the trees trapping warm air, and so the acers hold their leaves for that bit longer, extending the vibrancy of their display. Walking along the rides through a colourful confetti of leaves has a soothing effect, while the air smells distinctly clean and crisp.

There is a lot of structure here, provided by the evergreen yew and box, together with a mix of hollies, many of which are studded with berries that are beginning to colour. Three semi-mature birches with striking silver-white trunks are planted near the Sanctuary. These were given to His Royal Highness for his birthday by Her Majesty the Queen in 1997.

Some trees have great significance here, and will be retained whenever possible. Trees such as the *Fraxinus mandschurica,* or Manchurian ash, which is a rare tree confusingly also known as the Japanese oak, is a curious specimen with dark green branches. This tree has a special place in the Arboretum as it was planted and blessed by the Dalai Lama in May 1999.

It is during this time that any trees that were felled are cut into sizeable lengths and removed with the help of The Prince's two Suffolk Punches (heavy horses), Duke and Emperor. These two have now retired but heavy horses are still used across the estate because they cause less damage than a heavy wheeled vehicle, provided the ground is not

BELOW A glowing burst of yellow
*Acer palmatum* 'Sode-nishiki' catches
the low rays of the Autumn sun.

sodden. His Royal Highness also encourages the use of horses to remove timber from steep woodland, which can be easily damaged from the wheels of heavy vehicles.

Many cyclamen, daffodils, winter aconites and other bulbs will be planted or sown now on the Arboretum's floor. Each Autumn a new area will be cleared of any pernicious weeds and planted up with bulbs or corms. *Cyclamen coum* colonises well and some corms will go in, but seed is spread too, either brought in or collected from other areas in the garden. Winter aconites (*Eranthis hyemalis*) have a reputation for being difficult to spread from dried tubers and are easier to establish from fresh seed. When the green seedheads ripen, they can be gathered and distributed to new areas.

There are quite large volumes of squirrels, pheasants and rabbits who, during a long cold Winter, relish a snack of newly planted bulbs. Daffodils are given a wide berth by most rodents, as they are toxic, but the others are highly vulnerable to predation in their first Winter. The newly planted areas are covered with fruit cage netting, laid flat on the ground and pegged in place. It is removed after the bulbs have finished their first growing cycle and have gone dormant the following Summer.

Prince Charles is currently extending areas of shrub planting to provide more cover and significance to the area. *Aucuba japonica*, the spotted laurel with irregular yellow splodges on its evergreen leaves, has been increased

in quantity, with new groups being extensively planted recently in the Autumn. This is vulnerable to Muntjac deer, which are increasing in numbers dramatically as they have no fixed breeding season, unlike other deer, and so they reproduce all year round. They will quickly munch a cluster of shrubs to the ground and they are particularly partial to aucubas.

Other shrubs that are progressively planted here are groups of camellias, hydrangeas, osmanthus, magnolias and azaleas. All new plantings receive a heavy mulch now, to retain moisture and suppress any competitive vegetation.

Wandering through the Arboretum on a bracing November day, you see the beautifully mellow, honey-coloured Sanctuary at the end of a wide ride, lit by spangles of cool, low Winter light. This structure was built to mark the Millennium and as a thanksgiving to God. Now, 14 years on, this clay-lump building, which was created from local materials (subsoil, chalk and chopped straw) has very much settled into its clearing.

His Royal Highness has introduced many of his favourite plants on the walkway up to this personal and private space since it was finished; azaleas hug the glade, and now their Autumn colours of purples and reds shed rapidly after repeated cold spells. Near the door the leaves of a favourite maple, *Acer palmatum* 'Shindeshojo', turn reddish-orange before dropping, while ferns maintain some colour where they have colonised in cracks near the walls.

A carving above the door reads: '*Lighten our darkness, we beseech thee, O Lord*', and Tibetan bells hang around the outside of the building. At Christmas, Kevin Lomas, the Houseman, puts up welcoming swags of foliage around the outside, where they stay until Easter. The Sanctuary is an important place of contemplation, and adds a restful yet charming air to this pleasant and peaceful part of Highgrove. As one visitor aptly expressed it, 'The saying "One is nearer to God in a garden than anywhere else on Earth" sprang to mind.'

# Sundial Garden

In November, this garden is a peaceful space, and due to its sheltered position and south-facing orientation, His Royal Highness often enjoys sitting here to take in the serene and tranquil surroundings. The huge antique pots that are sited in the two smaller box-edged beds near the terrace look resplendent planted with immaculately tended roses.

The groundcover rose, *Rosa* 'Grouse', has its shoots carefully pulled down all around the outside of the pots, which encourages them to flower more profusely. These roses are vigorous and spread with delicate pale-pink single flowers. They repeat flower well, but even when out of flower the perfectly trained and arranged green stems, with colourful hips in Autumn, are stunning.

Another rose variety that is planted here is 'Highgrove', which was planted against the house wall in 2009. A beautiful short climber, it has blooms of a much sought-after dark garnet red colour. These large, old-fashioned double blooms continue through until December and have a delicate fragrance of raspberries. 'Highgrove' was bred by Peter Beales and he presented the rose to Camilla, Duchess of Cornwall, in 2009. Prince Charles had asked Peter for help in finding a rose to climb over the oak pavilion that sits over the remains of the old cedar, which resulted in this spectacular new climber.

The protective yew hedges that enclose the Sundial Garden manipulate the light so that shafts stream through the 'windows', making the yew on either side seem black by contrast. The hedges also temper the winds, helping the last of the roses to withstand less pleasant days, and making the job of deadheading very much more enjoyable.

Another feature of this garden is the magnificent stone table, made in Italy. In recent years, the table has been left outside every Winter; before then, it was not thought to be able to endure this climate with our many freeze-thaw cycles through the Winter and Spring. As stone is a natural material, it can sometimes behave unpredictably and different stones have differing degrees of durability. However, the table has come through several extreme Winters (notably 2011) totally unscathed.

At the end of the Sundial Garden furthest from the house, which runs towards the Kitchen Garden, the hornbeam avenue is visible. This avenue was originally planted with the crab apple *Malus* 'John Downie', which had been suggested by Lady Salisbury. She thought these would be best here due to the fact that it had usable fruits to line the walk to the Kitchen Garden, and is thought by many to be the best of the fruiting crabs, with its large, conical orange-red fruits that arrive in Autumn. In addition,

in Spring, the trees are laden with masses of white flowers, which the bees find irresistible.

In 1993, however, it was noticed that the trees were looking sick. The Royal Horticultural Society (of which the Queen is patron) was contacted and Pippa Greenwood, who was then an advisor, diagnosed that they were infected with scab, a fungal disease. In an avenue of trees, when some look sick and fail, not only is it a worry that the problem will spread, but the visual impact is lost. So the decision was made to replace them, and now a fine, thriving row of fastigiate hornbeams (*Carpinus betulus* 'Fastigiata') line the path instead. Prince Charles settled on these as he had admired some that had caught his eye while travelling around the outskirts of Oxford. These robust trees fit in well with the natural feel of the Meadow, are elegant, and do not cast too much shade over the myriad wild flowers that line this much-loved walkway.

Prince Charles takes on a very practical role in his garden. He receives regular weekly reports from his Head Gardener, which explain what has been done that week and queries new aspects, such as when would HRH like to set out the new border, or what would he like to replace a particular plant with? These questions are answered in great detail, with comments written beside each item with his famous red pen. Included, too, are reminders to do specific jobs that are becoming urgent.

Highgrove is very much Prince Charles's garden, and through his work in it and passion for it he has become an accomplished gardener. He knows the plants and their history better than anyone, quickly noticing if something is ailing or needs repairing and swift to ensure that what needs to be done is done, while also constantly evolving and refreshing its appearance.

LEFT Urns planted with *Helichrysum petiolare* stand outside the entrance to the Sundial Garden.

ABOVE The Prince joked that perhaps this should be renamed 'The Ego Garden', after four sculptors presented him with his likeness.

# Kitchen Garden

Early in the month of November, the gardeners are busy harvesting spinach, lettuce, carrots, beetroot and basketfuls of apples and pears. Later in the month, a heavy frost can change the scene, causing cascades of leaves to suddenly drop.

Just before the Winter weather-change, there is a race to get all the tender and vulnerable plants gathered or put safely under cover. The last of the potatoes have generally been lifted and stored by now, carefully packed into brown paper bags and set in the apple store. Some might be left in the ground until Christmas; usually they are safe like this, as the really severe weather tends to hold off until January.

The red and white onions are also kept in crates in the apple store, but some of the root crops – carrots, beetroot and parsnips – are left in the ground where they are protected from frost. In hard Winters, the gardeners may straw over the rows to help insulate them from more extreme cold.

The asparagus foliage offers a contribution of colours, as its delicate ferny leaves turn from green to a brilliant, buttery yellow before they are cut to the ground for the Winter, after the plant has absorbed the nutrients from the leaves.

In order to grow hearty vegetables, different organic strategies are employed to keep the non-beneficial bugs and any diseases at low levels. His Royal Highness has felt for many years that 'the endless use of chemicals was unsustainable', and aims to improve the health of the soil as a priority. The way to do this 'is to improve the organic matter in the soil to increase the humus and the worms and encourage the mycorrhizal activity'.

Until very recently, Dennis Brown had been in charge of the Kitchen Garden since 1984. He was a hugely keen and successful amateur vegetable grower before he became a professional. Dennis found it easy to grow organically as he had learnt the art from his father in the

The linked crab apple tree branches form a golden crown in Autumn.

years before the multitude of synthetic fertilisers and chemicals that are now on offer were available. Having built up many years' experience running arguably the most well-known organic vegetable garden in the world, Dennis is generous with sharing his knowledge.

His tricks of the trade include feeding plants in pots with comfrey tea, which is made on site at Highgrove. This concentrated liquid plant food is very effective and simple to make. The comfrey plant is known for its ability to store high levels of nutrients in its fleshy, bristly leaves and stems. The leaves are harvested up to three times a year and are often made into liquid plant food or added directly to the compost heap or potato, bean or sweet pea trenches.

At this time of year when the vegetables and flowers are more subdued, other enticing elements are quick to grab your attention. Four fabulous three-metre high, immaculately trimmed yew topiary pieces add elegance and contrast with the rows of the rather more humble vegetables. There is a fine bronze relief of 'The Green Man', which was created by the sculptor Nicholas Dimbleby and is inscribed with '*Genus Loci*', meaning 'Spirit of the Place', fixed to one wall. Two magnificently tall stone finials, carved by Simon Verity, sit on each side of the southern gateway and were a gift from Italian friends of The Prince.

Rosemary
*Rosmarinus officinalis*

# DECEMBER

'The anatomy and structure of the garden can be seen at its best in December. All the yew hedges and topiary shapes look crisp and clean cut, thanks to the skill and application of the garden staff. The pleached hornbeams on each side of the Thyme Walk are squared off and shipshape, while the frost has removed the last of the clinging, Autumn leaves from the trees. Early snow can bring icing sugar-covered enchantment to the geometric heart of the garden. The birds fall silent, the trees and plants rest from their divinely ordained labours on our behalf and the great mystery of life itself is ready to be renewed all over again …'

As the year draws to a close, the sharp lines of Highgrove's yew hedges embellish the views of many different parts of the garden; they look sharper now and even better in a more naked landscape where they reign supreme. Many guests visit the Orchard Room at this time of year, which looks enchanting set into the Cotswold landscape when covered in a white blanket of frost or even snow, for the resplendent Christmas shopping. The Terrace Garden is furnished in its Winter guise, too, and the view from the house highlights the dark topiary shapes which are arranged in pots to supplement other evergreens in the foreground. Stepping out onto the stone steps of the terrace from the house, the view to the Dovecote is now clear and neatly framed by lines of naked lime trunks. The house at Highgrove looked stark among its bare surroundings when Prince Charles first arrived, but now more than 30 years on, even in December, the building looks warm, inviting and full of life.

## Orchard Room

The Orchard Room is the arrival point for many guests and on a cold December morning, a more welcoming place cannot be imagined. Upon approaching the Orchard Room (which is dedicated to Paddy Whiteland), your eye is drawn to a row of stone columns supporting a low Cotswold stone roof that covers the entrance. There is nothing austere about this building; the steep pitch of the stone-tiled roof and the use of local materials help it sit comfortably in its rural surroundings. The thoughtful and clever detailing inside and out has been designed to make guests feel relaxed and at home.

Charles Morris was asked by His Royal Highness to design the building in 1998, to accommodate the increasing number of visitors who come from all over the world to see Highgrove's astounding gardens and often to hear about organic farming and His Royal Highness's gardening practices. Morris is a surveyor who has had a wealth of experience working with notable historic buildings as well as cutting-edge contemporary buildings.

The Orchard Room now welcomes almost 40,000 visitors every year, as well as many more who come to the large number of events and receptions that Prince Charles holds for the charities and causes he lends his support to. The Orchard Room was also used for Prince Charles's fiftieth and sixtieth birthday parties.

Choosing the best position – one close to the main house and with a short direct link to the garden – was the first decision. As the Orchard Room is approached from the Main (rear) Drive, you first see the newly planted Transylvanian Meadow in the foreground. The hedge in the field next to it has been immaculately cut and laid by Prince Charles and there are frequently cattle grazing here and in the surrounding pastures. It was decided to position the new building so the visitors could walk through the charming, enclosed Orchard before entering the garden proper. You usually enter via the Indian Gate, which was formed to create this important link between the entrance and the garden.

The Orchard Room is inspired by the Arts and Crafts movement in many ways: there are wooden gutters (with copper linings) and the decorations and features are part of the structure rather than being bolted on – beautifully illustrated by the impressive, warm, friendly fireplace in the entrance hall. One of the most notable features of the Orchard Room is the wide stone columns that support the covered entrance, directly outside the front doors.

The purpose of these columns is not just to form a convenient covered space, but also to temper the strong south light that would have flooded the room. A dim room is always more atmospheric than a bright one, and it was thought to be important to create a restful, convivial ambience. The columns (albeit slightly different) continue inside the building and help to merge the inside and outside spaces.

The space outside the building is as important and well used as its interior. The wide doors allow the terrace to accommodate guests in this warm, south-facing garden, which backs on to the Carriage Wash. There are two arbours here, with beautiful oak shakes for the roof, which were part of one of His Royal Highness's gardens at the Chelsea Flower Show. The quote by William Blake, '*To See a World in a Grain of Sand*' is carved in the wood in blue.

Nearby is the Highgrove shop, which sells many of the same plants that are also grown in the garden, beautifully displayed on the paving at peak visiting times. In Winter, the shop also sells gifts for the holiday season, which combined with the warm atmosphere of the Orchard Room, gets one in the holiday spirit very quickly.

PREVIOUS The hedges and topiary are at their best in the dead of Winter, especially when seen from the impressive west-facing vista from the Terrace Garden.

LEFT The Orchard Room, near the house, was built to welcome the many visitors to Highgrove's gardens.

RIGHT The arbour in the space right outside the Orchard Room is from the Chelsea Flower Show garden in 1998.

# Terrace Garden

The Terrace Garden is a high-profile part of Highgrove – it is on show from the French doors and in December the view of it from the reception room is much enjoyed by His Royal Highness's many seasonal visitors. On crisp December mornings when there is frost or snow, the electrifying panoramic view of the icy-clad and beautifully shaped topiary hedges, the hornbeam trees and the many varied, classically cut topiary shapes lifts the spirit. It is breathtaking views such as these, which change by the hour, the month and the year, with variations in light, weather, plants and atmosphere, that make England one of the most exciting (and challenging) places to create a garden, especially one as grand as Highgrove.

On the two outer corners of the Terrace are two remarkable stone pavilions. Before they were built, two Gothic chairs, made by the joiners at Chatsworth (which are now located in the pavilions) were positioned in the corner where Prince Charles used to sit and write his speeches. In 1987 The Prince decided to ask the architect Willie Bertram to design two small pepperpot buildings

LEFT and BELOW You can just see the gilded finial atop the 10-metre-high obelisk, built in memorium to a felled, ancient cedar of Lebanon.

at the outer corners of the Terrace after Prince Charles was 'inspired by two such buildings at Cranborne Manor in Dorset, though theirs were far larger'. These structures were intended 'to emphasise the limits of that charming garden', as Willie puts it. At this time, the yew hedges were getting well into their stride (now 1.5 metres high) and began to divide the former park into a wonderful series of outdoor rooms. His Royal Highness felt vulnerable sitting with his back to the lawn while concentrating on his writing and so wanted two tiny buildings to act 'as overcoats'.

Sitting in the shelter of the intimately-sized 'beehives' you have special framed views of the magnificent topiary on the Lawn. On the back wall and recessed into the yellow render are three highly decorative, richly coloured tiles. These were based on choisya leaves, designed by Prince Charles, and made by the architect Christopher Alexander. They are highly textured and richly glazed in reds, blues, greens and brown. On the windowsills are special mementoes, porcelain bamboo stems, glazed leaves and candles. It is these little details around the grounds that make Highgrove, unlike many gardens of this grand scale, feel lived in. It is a personal space and very much one that is enjoyed and appreciated by its proud owner.

## Hedges

Many stunning views of Highgrove feature the distinctive topiarised yew hedge that encircles the estate. Despite the wealth of amazing gardens in this country, nowhere has such a notably embellished hedge as the one at Highgrove. It stretches to a length of over half a kilometre of beautifully maintained, thick, dark green hedging that wraps around the west and south elevations of the house, forming a series of contrasting spaces around and within it.

It is fascinating to watch a garden evolve, and none more so than over the 30-plus years that The Prince has been developing Highgrove. When Prince Charles first laid out the hedge in 1982, using canes and string in the open Parkland to try to achieve the desired layout of the various spaces, it would have been difficult for anyone to visualise just how these organic walls would define these splendid gardens so dramatically. Even when the bushy plants had been planted during that Winter and began to define the boundaries of the Sundial Garden, Terrace Garden, Main Lawn and Cottage Garden, it was difficult to foresee quite what a starring role the hedges would play.

The prime reason for the instigation of the hedges was for privacy. The house and parts of the garden could be seen through the long lenses of the press when The Prince first moved in, which prevented it being a place he could relax and enjoy with family and friends without intrusion. Lawrence Johnston's garden at Hidcote Manor in Gloucestershire (started in 1903), which has a magnificent framework of disciplined hedges and strong axial views, was, and is still, a strong influence on many budding gardeners, including Prince Charles. There and here, the hedges were employed to define the spaces, create superb backdrops to plant against, add shelter, focus views and create more intimacy.

Their strong shapes with balls of yew, alcoves, piers, birds, arches, pyramids, swoops and swags create a dramatic visual interest to delight and amuse, even in the Winter months when other planting has died back until Spring. When backlit by warm Winter light, golden halos appear around the silhouetted shapes, and shafts of gold spill through the arches. Most importantly, the hedges pull together all the

various spaces, giving a pleasing sense of unity to a garden that has many different and fascinating parts.

When the yews were about 1.5 to 1.8 metres high, Prince Charles decided he would like to have some windows cut through. The Prince duly asked Roy Strong to come and advise, which he did and surveyed the hedges, later producing several sketch ideas of how they might be elaborated. He showed different treatments in the various stretches but was extremely concerned that they were planted slightly off the axis so possible viewpoints would not line up. It is often the case with outdoor spaces that what you perceive to be perfect squares, rectangles or other geometrical shapes are in fact some way off perfect proportions. Sir Roy Strong's design took this on board and no one is any the wiser of its imperfections now.

His Royal Highness noticed that the security men had to walk some way to go around all the hedging, making their regular routes far longer than necessary. So he decided to cut spaces in strategic places and a few eye-catching gates were designed for the new gaps.

Sir Roy undertook the first clipping of the hedge, assisted by Wilf, his assistant, who helped him with the topiary and hedges in his own garden. They came back for the next three years and repeated the performance, arriving early, leaving late. After this time, the pattern was established and the Highgrove gardening team took over. The hedge is cut using mechanical hedge cutters and sharp shears between August and November, after the main flush of growth, so it looks sharp and crisp throughout the Winter.

Sir Roy returned to survey the hedge in 2012, by which time his pencil sketch from 1988, which His Royal Highness still has at Highgrove, had metamorphosed into perfect, living hedges, 'I was', he said, 'rather proud of it.' And rightly so.

# The House

The walls of the house that adjoin the Sundial Garden have largely lost their leaves now, the foliage from the wisteria has finally been shed and soon it will be heavily cut back to remove most of last year's growth, right down to its permanent framework of branches. The jasmine trained on the front of the single-storey bay is *Jasminum officinale* f. *affine*, a particularly splendid form of this highly scented climber, which remains almost evergreen in mild Winters, offering a splash of colour against the stone. The large, evergreen *Viburnum tinus* that nestles against the house walls blooms erratically from December to April, and the tight rosy-pink buds open to produce flattened heads of stoic, white flowers that seem to look cheerful and perfect whatever the weather decides to throw at them.

Other evergreens, including a huge *Choisya ternata*, euonymus and ceanothus, hug the base of the building, softening the transition between the vertical walls and paving, helping to anchor the house into the garden even through the Winter months. They also serve to hide the large timber barrel that collects the grey water harvested from the house, which is useful for irrigating the containers and delphiniums in the Summer months. The evergreens are also vital habitats for birds, small mammals and insects that appreciate the extra cover and warmth they provide.

The west-facing elevation of the house that looks over the Terrace Garden is the outlook that the majority of visitors see as they arrive; few can pass by without pausing to admire the view of the magnificent Thyme Walk and Lily Pool Garden, and in December this strong vista perfectly connects the house with its world-famous garden.

The warm ashlar stone of the house is covered with variegated ivy, which is allowed to venture no further than the top of the second-floor windows, a line to which it is clipped tightly during the Winter months. Clipping it every year keeps the ivy in its juvenile form and protects the stonework from extreme temperatures. Its dense evergreen cloak of leaves also provides a wonderful habitat for birds and insects. There is also a huge *Magnolia grandiflora* on the right-hand side, which has now just passed the height of the second-floor window. This giant (with large glossy, evergreen leaves) is left to grow almost unchecked. This substantial wall shrub is often at its best when grown on houses of similar large proportions, both complementing and showing each other off to their best.

As another year comes to an end, the garden goes on, changing, maturing and ensuring its dramatic presence for another year. The work continues, whatever the weather, and the new year brings new hope, new plans and new vistas in a garden that continues to develop and reflect the vision and passion of its dedicated gardener.

LEFT The garden is increasingly spectacular as it matures, as new developments are happening every year.

ABOVE The Thyme Walk is almost unrecognisable from just a few months previous, when the colourful cushions of thyme were buzzing with bees and golden Summer growth lit up the yew.

# PLANT LISTING

Campanula lactiflora 'Prichard's Variety' — Herbaceous Perennial
Campanula punctata 'Rubriflora' — Herbaceous Perennial
Ceanothus 'Puget Blue' — Evergreen Shrub
Cornus 'Gloria Birkett' — Deciduous Shrub
Cornus alba 'Elegantissima' — Deciduous Shrub
Cotinus coggygria 'Royal Purple' — Deciduous Shrub
Delphinium 'Cassius' — Herbaceous Perennial
Delphinium 'Faust' — Herbaceous Perennial
Deutzia × elegantissima — Deciduous Shrub
Echinacea purpurea Bressingham hybrids — Herbaceous Perennial
Eryngium × tripartitum — Herbaceous Perennial
Geranium 'Ann Folkard' — Herbaceous Perennial
Geranium × magnificum 'Rosemoor' — Herbaceous Perennial
Heuchera 'Leuchtkäfer' — Perennial
Hydrangea 'Annabelle' — Deciduous Shrub
Ilex aquifolium 'Ferox Argentea' — Evergreen Shrub
Ilex × altaclerensis 'Golden King' — Evergreen Tree
Iris 'Sable' — Perennial
Juniperus scopulorum 'Skyrocket' — Evergreen Tree
Lonicera × purpusii 'Winter Beauty' — Deciduous Shrub
Lythrum virgatum 'Dropmore Purple' — Herbaceous Perennial
Nepeta racemosa 'Walker's Low' — Herbaceous Perennial
Phlox paniculata 'Bright Eyes' — Herbaceous Perennial
Salvia nemorosa 'Lubecca' — Herbaceous Perennial
Sedum 'Vera Jameson' — Herbaceous Perennial
Staphylea pinnata — Deciduous Tree
Taxus baccata 'Fastigiata' — Evergreen Tree

## NEW COTTAGE GARDEN

Acer palmatum cultivars — Deciduous Tree
Acer pensylvanicum — Deciduous Tree
Actinidia deliciosa 'Hayward' — Deciduous Climber
Angelica archangelica — Biennial
Brunnera macrophylla — Herbaceous Perennial
Cephalaria gigantea — Herbaceous Perennial
Chimonanthus praecox — Deciduous Shrub
Choisya × dewitteana — Evergreen Shrub
Choisya ternata Sundance — Evergreen Shrub
Hydrangea quercifolia — Deciduous Shrub
Ligularia The Rocket — Herbaceous Perennial
Ligustrum japonicum 'Rotundifolium' — Evergreen Shrub
Liriodendron tulipifera 'Aureomarginatum' — Deciduous Tree
Lysimachia ciliata 'Firecracker' — Herbaceous Perennial
Lysimachia punctata — Herbaceous Perennial
Maclaya cordata — Herbaceous Perennial
Magnolia × loebneri 'Leonard Messel' — Deciduous Tree
Morus nigra — Deciduous Tree
Philadelphus 'Belle Etoile' — Deciduous Shrub
Philadelphus 'Silberregen' — Deciduous Shrub
Philadelphus 'Snow Velvet' — Deciduous Shrub
Phlomis russeliana — Herbaceous Perennial
Sambucus 'Black Beauty' — Deciduous Shrub
Thalictrum delavayi 'White Cloud' — Herbaceous Perennial
Viburnum × globosum 'Jermyns Globe' — Evergreen Shrub
Viburnum × hillieri — Evergreen Shrub
Zantedeschia aethiopica — Herbaceous Perennial

## OAK PAVILION BED

Ceanothus 'Puget Blue' — Evergreen Shrub
Hosta 'Patriot' — Herbaceous Perennial
Hosta 'Sum and Substance' — Herbaceous Perennial
Magnolia stellata 'Rosea' — Deciduous Shrub
Narcissus minor 'Pumilis' — Bulb
Philadelphus coronarius — Evergreen Shrub
Philadelphus × virginalis 'Minnesota Snowflake' — Deciduous Shrub
Rosa 'Highgrove' — Deciduous Climber
Rosa 'Home Sweet Home' — Deciduous Climber
Wisteria floribunda 'Macrobotrys' — Deciduous Climber

## PERGOLA

Clematis Avant-garde — Deciduous Climber
Clematis 'Comtesse de Bouchard' — Deciduous Climber

Clematis 'Madame Julia Correvon' — Deciduous Climber
Clematis 'Perle d'Azur' — Deciduous Climber
Clematis 'M. Koster' — Deciduous Climber
Clematis 'Polish Spirit' — Deciduous Climber
Clematis Sugar Candy — Deciduous Climber
Rosa 'Bantry Bay' — Deciduous Climber
Rosa 'Ethel' — Deciduous Climber
Rosa 'François Juranville' — Deciduous Climber
Rosa 'Minnehaha' — Deciduous Climber
Rosa 'Shot Silk' — Deciduous Climber
Rosa Sir Paul Smith — Deciduous Climber
Rosa 'Veilchenblau' — Deciduous Climber
Rosa 'Wedding day' — Deciduous Climber
Rosa mulliganii — Deciduous Climber
Wisteria floribunda 'Macrobotrys' — Deciduous Climber
Wisteria sinensis — Deciduous Climber

## MEDITERRANEAN GARDEN

Asphodeline lutea — Herbaceous Perennial
Campanula hofmanii — Herbaceous Perennial
Cistus × argenteus 'Peggy Sammons' — Evergreen Shrub
Cistus × argenteus 'Silver Pink' — Evergreen Shrub
Cistus creticus — Evergreen Shrub
Cistus ladanifer — Evergreen Shrub
Cistus monspeliensis — Evergreen Shrub
Crinum × powellii — Hardy Bulb
Geranium psilostemon — Herbaceous Perennial
Indigofera amblyantha — Deciduous Shrub
Indigofera gerardiana — Deciduous Shrub
Koelreuteria paniculata — Deciduous Tree
Lamium maculatum Pink Chablis — Perennial Groundcover
Lavatera × clementii 'Burgundy Wine' — Deciduous Shrub
Lavendula angustifolia 'Munstead' — Evergreen Shrub
Lychnis coronaria — Biennial
Malus trilobata — Deciduous Tree
Muscari armeniacum 'Early Giant' — Hardy Bulb
Nepeta racemosa 'Walkers Low' — Herbaceous Perennial
Perovskia 'Blue Spire' — Deciduous Shrub
Philadelphus maculatus 'Mexican Jewel' — Deciduous Shrub
Philadelphus 'Starbright' — Deciduous Shrub
Polemonium caeruleum — Herbaceous Perennial
Stachys byzantina (syn. lanata) — Perennial Groundcover
Teucrium × lucidrys — Evergreen Shrub

## INDIAN GATE, POTS AND YELLOW BORDER

Acer platanoides Princeton Gold — Deciduous Tree
Aquilegia chrysantha 'Yellow Queen' — Herbaceous perennial
Catalpa bignonioides 'Aurea' — Deciduous Tree
Clematis Reflections — Deciduous Climber
Clematis Wisley — Deciduous Climber
Clematis 'Elizabeth' — Deciduous Climber
Corydalis 'Canary Feathers' — Herbaceous perennial
Digitalis grandiflora — Herbaceous perennial
Doronicum caucasicum 'Magnificum' — Herbaceous perennial
Epimedium × versicolor 'Sulphureum' — Herbaceous perennial
Fraxinus ornus — Deciduous Tree
Leptinella squalida — Perennial Ground cover
Lilium leichtlinii — Bulb
Mahonia 'Winter Sun' — Evergreen Shrub
Narcissus 'Trena' — Bulb
Narcissus 'Warbler' — Bulb
Parrotia persica — Deciduous Tree
Rosa 'Cécile Brünner' — Deciduous Climber
Rosa 'Jude the Obscure' — Deciduous Climber
Selaginella lepidophylla — Perennial Ground cover
Soleirolia soleirolii — Perennial Ground cover

## BUTTRESS GARDEN

*Pink and Yellow in March/April bed*

Aquilegia 'Rose Queen' — Herbaceous Perennial
Bergenia 'Overture' — Evergreen Perennial
Camellia × williamsii 'Debbie' — Evergreen Shrub

| | |
|---|---|
| *Crataegus laecigata* 'Paul's Scarlet' | Deciduous Tree |
| *Daphne odora* 'Aureomarginata' | Evergreen Shrub |
| *Forsythia* 'Golden Nugget' | Deciduous Shrub |
| *Forsythia × intermedia* 'Lynwood Variety' | Deciduous Shrub |
| *Narcissus* 'Hawera' | Bulb |
| *Primula bulleyana* | Evergreen Perennial |
| *Primula japonica* 'Miller's Crimson' | Herbaceous Perennial |
| *Ribes sanguineum* 'King Edward VII' | Deciduous Shrub |
| *Ribes sanguineum* 'Pulborough Scarlet' | Deciduous Shrub |
| *Viburnum carlcephalum* | Evergreen Shrub |

*Yellow and Blue in June bed*

| | |
|---|---|
| *Agapanthus* 'Navy Blue' | Herbaceous Perennial |
| *Aquilegia* 'Blue Star' | Herbaceous Perennial |
| *Buddleja × weyeriana* 'Moonlight' | Deciduous Shrub |
| *Buddleja davidii* 'Blue Horizon' | Deciduous Shrub |
| *Campanula persicifolia* 'Telham Beauty' | Herbaceous Perennial |
| *Ceanothus* 'Puget Blue' | Evergreen Shrub |
| *Cornus alba* 'Aurea' | Deciduous Shrub |
| *Cytisus scoparius* 'Golden Cascade' | Deciduous Shrub |
| *Cytisus × praecox* 'Allgold' | Deciduous Shrub |
| *Delphinium* Bluebird Group | Herbaceous Perennial |
| *Delphinium* King Arthur Group | Herbaceous Perennial |
| *Digitalis grandiflora* 'Carillon' | Herbaceous Perennial |
| *Euphorbia characias* subsp. *wulfenii* 'Lambrook Gold' | Herbaceous Perennial |
| *Iris pseudoacorus* 'Variegata' | Herbaceous Perennial |
| *Lupinus* 'Chandelier' | Herbaceous Perennial |
| *Lupinus* 'The Governor' | Herbaceous Perennial |
| *Philadelphus coronarius* 'Aurea' | Deciduous Shrub |
| *Spartium junceum* | Deciduous Shrub |

*Red, Pink and Purple in September/October bed*

| | |
|---|---|
| *Anemone × hybrida* 'Honorine Jobert' | Herbaceous Perennial |
| *Anemone × hybrida* 'Königin Charlotte' | Herbaceous Perennial |
| *Aster × frikartii* 'Mönch' | Herbaceous Perennial |
| *Buddleja* 'Miss Ruby | Deciduous Shrub |
| *Clerodendron bungei* | Deciduous Shrub |
| *Euonymus alatus* | Deciduous Shrub |
| *Fuchsia* 'Mrs Popple' | Deciduous Shrub |
| *Fuchsia magellanica* 'Angel's Teardrop' | Deciduous Shrub |
| *Hydrangea macrophylla* 'Geoffrey Chadbund' | Deciduous Shrub |
| *Hydrangea macrophylla* 'King George' | Deciduous Shrub |
| *Lobelia × speciosa* 'Hadspen Purple' | Herbaceous Perennial |

LAUREL TUNNEL

| | |
|---|---|
| *Blechnum chilense* | Evergreen Fern. |
| *Daphne odora* 'Aureomarginata' | Evergreen Shrub |
| *Daphne × translatlantica* Eternal Fragrance | Evergreen Shrub |
| *Digitalis grandiflora* 'Carillon' | Herbaceous Perennial |
| *Digitalis purpurea* | Biennial |
| *Digitalis* 'Strawberry Crush' | Herbaceous Perennial |
| *Dryopteris affinis* | Semi-Evergreen Fern |
| *Dryopteris affinis* 'Stableri' | Semi-Evergreen Fern |
| *Dryopteris atrata* | Semi-Evergreen Fern |
| *Dryopteris dilatata* 'Crispa Whiteside' | Semi-Evergreen Fern |
| *Dryopteris filix-mas* | Deciduous Fern |
| *Dryopteris filix-mas* 'Cristata Martindale' | Deciduous Fern |
| *Dryopteris wallichiana* | Deciduous Fern |
| *Liriodendron tulipifera* | Deciduous Tree |
| *Maianthemum racemosum* | Herbaceous Perennial |
| *Pachysandra terminalis* 'Green Carpet' | Evergreen Shrub |
| *Polygonatum × hybridum* | Herbaceous Perennial |

ORCHARD

| | |
|---|---|
| Apple 'Devonshire Buckland' | Deciduous Tree |
| Apple 'Duchess's Favourite' | Deciduous Tree |
| Apple 'First and Last' | Deciduous Tree |
| Apple 'Lamb Abbey Pearmain' | Deciduous Tree |
| Apple 'London Pearmain' | Deciduous Tree |
| Apple 'Rivers Nonsuch' | Deciduous Tree |
| *Muscari* 'Early Giant' | Hardy Bulb |
| *Nepeta × faassenii* | Herbaceous Perennial |

CARPET GARDEN

| | |
|---|---|
| *Astrantia* 'Hadspen Blood' | Herbaceous Perennial |
| *Clematis* Vesuvius | Deciduous climber |
| *Clematis* Petit Faucon | Deciduous climber |
| *Clematis* Rosemoor | Deciduous climber |
| *Clematis* 'Ville de Lyon' | Deciduous climber |
| *Cupressus sempervirens* 'Stricta' | Evergreen Tree |
| *Eupatorium rugosum* 'Chocolate' | Herbaceous Perennial |
| *Geranium* Rozanne (syn. 'Jolly Bee') | Herbaceous Perennial |
| *Lathyrus sativus* var. *azureus* | Annual |
| *Lobelia × speciosa* 'Vedrariensis' | Herbaceous Perennial |
| *Olea europaea* | Evergreen Tree |
| *Pelargonium* 'Purple Unique' | Half hardy perennials |
| *Rosa* 'Alfred Colomb' | Deciduous Shrub |
| *Rosa* Bonica | Deciduous Shrub |
| *Rosa* 'Duchesse de Montebello' | Deciduous Shrub |
| *Rosa* 'Europeana' | Deciduous Shrub |
| *Rosa* 'Roundelay' | Deciduous Climber |
| *Rosa* 'Sander's White Rambler' | Deciduous Climber |
| *Rosa* 'Souvenir du Docteur Jamain' | Deciduous Climber |
| *Rosa* 'The Garland' | Deciduous Climber |
| *Rosa gallica* var. *officinalis* | Deciduous Shrub |
| *Salvia candelabra* | Evergreen shrub |
| *Silene fimbriata* | Herbaceous Perennial |
| *Trachelospermum jasminoides* | Evergreen Climber |
| *Viola* 'Martin' | Annual |
| *Citrus × microcarpa* | Evergreen Tree |

LILY POOL GARDEN

| | |
|---|---|
| *Acca sellowiana* (syn. *Feijoa sellowiana*) | Evergreen Shrub |
| *Agapanthus* 'Navy Blue' | Herbaceous Perennial |
| *Allium caeruleum* | Bulb |
| *Ceanothus* 'Puget Blue' | Evergreen Shrub |
| *Geranium* Rozanne (syn. 'Jolly Bee') | Herbaceous Perennial |
| *Narcissus* 'Tête-à-tête' | Bulb |
| *Nymphaea* 'Charlene Strawn' | Aquatic Perennial |
| *Nymphaea* 'Rosy Morn' | Aquatic Perennial |
| *Nymphaea* 'White Sultan' | Aquatic Perennial |
| *Nymphaea* 'Yul Ling' | Aquatic Perennial |
| *Origanum vulgare* 'Aureum' | Herbaceous Perennial |
| *Perovskia* 'Blue Spire' | Deciduous Shrub |
| *Philadephus coronarius* 'Aureus' | Deciduous Shrub |
| *Primula denticulata* | Herbaceous Perennial |
| *Rosa* Elina | Deciduous Shrub |
| *Rosa* Grosvenor House | Deciduous Shrub |
| *Rosmarinus officinalis* | Evergreen Shrub |
| *Salvia forsskaolii* | Herbaceous Perennial |
| *Salvia patens* 'Cambridge Blue' | Half-hardy Perennial |
| *Thalictrum aquilegiifolium* | Herbaceous Perennial |

WILDFLOWER MEADOW

| | |
|---|---|
| *Allium hollandicum* 'Purple Sensation' | Bulb |
| *Anacamptis morio* (green winged orchid) | Native perennial |
| *Camassia quamash* (quamash) | Bulb |
| *Camassia leichtlinii* Caerulea Group | Bulb |
| *Centaurea nigra* (common knapweed) | Native perennial |
| *Dactylorhiza fuchsii* (common spotted orchid) | Native perennial |
| *Dactylorhiza praetermissa* (southern marsh orchid) | Native perennial |
| *Fritillaria meleagris* (snake's head fritillary) | Bulb |
| *Geranium pratense* (meadow cranesbill) | Native perennial |
| *Gladiolus byzantinus* | Bulb |
| *Knautia arvensis* (field scabious) | Native perennial |
| *Leontodon hispidus* (rough hawksbit) | Native perennial |
| *Leucanthemum vulgare* (moon daisy) | Native perennial |
| *Narcissus* 'Camilla Duchess of Cornwall' | Bulb |
| *Narcissus* 'Ice Follies' | Bulb |
| *Narcissus* 'February Gold' | Bulb |
| *Narcissus* 'February Silver' | Bulb |
| *Narcissus* 'Jenny' | Bulb |
| *Narcissus* var *recurvus* (old pheasants eye) | Bulb |
| *Narcissus pseudonarcissus* subsp. *pseudonarcissus* | Bulb |
| *Plantago lanceolata* (ribwort plantain) | Native perennial |

| | |
|---|---|
| *Primula veris* (Cowslip) | Native perennial |
| *Ranunculus acris* (Meadow Buttercup) | Native perennial |
| *Rhianthus minor* (Yellow Rattle) | Native Annual |
| *Tulipa sylvestris* | Bulb |

## STUMPERY

| | |
|---|---|
| *Acer palmatum* 'Bloodgood' | Deciduous Tree. |
| *Acer palmatum* var. *dissectum* 'Seiryū' | Deciduous Tree. |
| *Acer palmatum* 'Ōzakazuki' | Deciduous Tree. |
| *Actaea simplex* Atropurpurea Group | Herbaceous perennial |
| *Adiantum venustum* | Fern |
| *Allium nigrum* | Bulb |
| *Anemone blanda* blue-flowered | Bulb |
| *Arisaema formosanum* | Bulb |
| *Arisaema griffithii* | Bulb |
| *Camellia* 'Peach Blossom' | Evergreen Shrub |
| *Cotinus coggygria* | Deciduous Shrub |
| *Cyclamen hederifolium* | Bulb |
| *Cyclamen pseudoibericum* | Bulb |
| *Cyclamen repandum* | Bulb |
| *Daphne bholua* 'Jacqueline Postill' | Evergreen Shrub |
| *Davidia involucrata* | Deciduous Tree |
| *Dicentra spectablis* 'Alba' | Herbaceous Perennial |
| *Digitalis purpurea* Excelsior Group | Biennial |
| *Dryopteris affinis* 'Cristata' | Fern |
| *Dryopteris affinis* 'Grandiceps Askew' | Fern |
| *Dryopteris filix-mas* 'Cristata Martindale' | Fern |
| *Epimedium acuminatum* | Evergreen Perennial |
| *Eranthus hyemalis* | Bulb |
| *Erythronium* 'Pagoda' | Bulb |
| *Erythronium revolutum* 'Knightshayes Pink' | Bulb |
| *Euphorbia griffithii* 'Fireglow' | Herbaceous Perennial |
| *Fritillaria meleagris* | Bulb |
| *Galanthus* 'S. Arnott' | Bulb |
| *Galanthus nivalis* 'Flore Pleno' | Bulb |
| *Gunnera manicata* | Herbaceous Perennial |
| *Helleborus argutifolius* | Evergreen Perennial |
| *Helleborus* × *hybridus* Ashwood Garden Hybrids | Evergreen Perennial |
| *Hepatica nobilis* | Herbaceous Perennial |
| *Hosta* 'Domaine de Courson' | Herbaceous Perennial |
| *Hosta* 'Empress Wu' | Herbaceous Perennial |
| *Hosta* 'Halcyon' | Herbaceous Perennial |
| *Hosta* 'Liberty' | Herbaceous Perennial |
| *Hosta* 'Prince of Wales' | Herbaceous Perennial |
| *Hosta* 'Regal Splendor' | Herbaceous Perennial |
| *Hosta* 'Sum and Substance' | Herbaceous Perennial |
| *Hydrangea aspera* Villosa Group | Deciduous Shrub |
| *Iris chrysographes* | Herbaceous Perennial |
| *Iris foetidissima* var. *citrina* | Herbaceous Perennial |
| *Iris* × *robusta* 'Gerald Darby' | Herbaceous Perennial |
| *Kirengeshoma palmata* | Herbaceous Perennial |
| *Koelreuteria paniculata* | Deciduous Tree. |
| *Leucojum aestivum* 'Gravetye Giant' | Bulb |
| *Ligularia przewalkskii* | Herbaceous Perennial |
| *Lilium martagon* | Bulb |
| *Magnolia* 'Athene' | Deciduous Tree. |
| *Magnolia stellata* | Deciduous Shrub |
| *Mahonia* × *media* 'Charity' | Evergreen Shrub |
| *Muscari latifolium* | Bulb |
| *Narcissus* 'Jack Snipe' | Bulb |
| *Narcissus* 'Misty Glen' | Bulb |
| *Narcissus* 'Petrel' | Bulb |
| *Narcissus* 'Silver Chimes' | Bulb |
| *Paeonia rockii* | Deciduous Shrub |
| *Philadelphus coronarius* | Deciduous Shrub |
| *Prunus* 'Accolade' | Deciduous Tree. |
| *Quercus frainetto* | Deciduous Tree. |
| *Rheum palmatum* 'Atrosanguineum' | Herbaceous Perennial |
| *Rodgersia aesculifolia* | Herbaceous Perennial |
| *Ruscus aculeatus* | Evergreen Shrub |
| *Smyrnium perfoliatum* | Biennial |
| *Stachys macrantha* 'Superba' | Herbaceous Perennial |
| *Strobilanthes atropurpurea* | Herbaceous Perennial |

| | |
|---|---|
| *Telekia speciosa* | Herbaceous Perennial |
| *Tricyrtis formosana* | Herbaceous Perennial |

## LOWER ORCHARD

| | |
|---|---|
| Apple 'Discovery' | Deciduous Tree |
| Apple 'Herefordshire Russet' | Deciduous Tree |
| Crab-apple 'John Downie' | Deciduous Tree |
| Damson 'Merryweather' | Deciduous Tree |
| Damson 'Shropshire Prune' | Deciduous Tree |
| *Malus hupehensis* | Deciduous Tree |
| Medlar 'Nottingham' | Deciduous Tree |
| Pear 'Concorde' | Deciduous Tree |
| Pear 'Onward' | Deciduous Tree |
| Plum 'Marjorie's Seedling' | Deciduous Tree |
| Plum 'Yellow Egg' | Deciduous Tree |
| Quince 'Meech's Prolific' | Deciduous Tree |

## WINTERBOURNE GARDEN

| | |
|---|---|
| *Acer platinoides* Princeton Gold | Deciduous Tree |
| *Acradenia frankliniae* | Evergreen Shrub |
| *Blechnum chilense* | Fern |
| *Brunnera* 'Looking Glass' | Herbaceous Perennial |
| *Brunnera macrophylla* 'Hadspen Cream' | Herbaceous Perennial |
| *Cardamine quinquefolia* | Herbaceous Perennial |
| *Cardiocrinum giganteum* | Bulb |
| *Ceanothus* 'Puget Blue' | Evergreen Shrub |
| *Ceanothus* 'Skylark' | Evergreen Shrub |
| *Colchicum* 'The Giant' | Bulb |
| *Cornus* 'Eddie's White Wonder' | Deciduous Shrub |
| *Cornus* 'Norman Haddon' | Deciduous Shrub |
| *Cornus kousa* 'China Girl' | Deciduous Shrub |
| *Cornus kousa* 'Satomi' | Deciduous Shrub |
| *Cornus kousa* var. *chinensis* 'Claudia' | Deciduous Shrub |
| *Cornus kousa* var. *chinensis* 'Milky Way' | Deciduous Shrub |
| *Dahlia* 'Admiral Rawlings' | Herbaceous Perennial |
| *Dahlia imperialis* | Herbaceous Perennial |
| *Dicksonia antartica* | Fern |
| *Dicksonia fibrosa* | Fern |
| *Eryngium yuccifolium* | Evergreen Perennial |
| *Fascicularia bicolor* | Evergreen Perennial |
| *Griselinia littoralis* | Evergreen Shrub |
| *Gunnera manicata* | Herbaceous Perennial |
| *Hoheria sexstylosa* | Evergreen Tree |
| *Hydrangea paniculata* 'Brussels Lace' | Deciduous Shrub |
| *Hydrangea paniculata* 'Confetti' | Deciduous Shrub |
| *Hydrangea paniculata* 'Limelight' | Deciduous Shrub |
| *Hydrangea paniculata* Magical Fire | Deciduous Shrub |
| *Hydrangea paniculata* Sundae Fraise | Deciduous Shrub |
| *Impatiens tinctoria* subsp. *tinctoria* | Herbaceous Perennial |
| *Lilium martagon* | Bulb |
| *Liriodendron chinense* | Deciduous Tree |
| *Lobelia* × *speciosa* 'Vedrariensis' | Herbaceous Perennial |
| *Musa basjoo* | Herbaceous Perennial |
| *Narcisssus* 'Hawera' | Bulb |
| *Nothofagus antarctica* | Deciduous Tree |
| *Philadelphus* 'Belle Etoile' | Deciduous Shrub |
| *Philadelphus* 'Manteau d'Hermine' | Deciduous Shrub |
| *Philadelphus* 'Minnesota Snowflake' | Deciduous Shrub |
| *Philadelphus* 'Silberregen' | Deciduous Shrub |
| *Philadelphus* 'Snowbelle' | Deciduous Shrub |
| *Philadelphus maculatus* 'Mexican Jewel' | Deciduous Shrub |
| *Podocarpus salignus* | Evergreen Tree |
| *Primula pulverulenta* | Herbaceous Perennial |
| *Pulmonaria* 'Blue Ensign' | Evergreen Perennial |
| *Pulmonaria* Opal | Evergreen Perennial |
| *Symphytum* 'All Gold' | Evergreen Perennial |
| *Tellima grandiflora* 'Purpurea' | Evergreen Perennial |
| *Tetrapanax papyrifer* | Deciduous Shrub |
| *Trachycarpus fortunei* | Evergreen Shrub |
| *Wollemia nobilis* | Evergreen Tree |
| *Zantedeschia aethiopica* | Herbaceous Perennial |

| | |
|---|---|
| *Allium cowanii* | Bulb |
| *Arisaema sikokianum* | Bulb |
| *Arisaema speciosum* | Bulb |
| *Galium odoratum* | Herbaceous Perennial |
| *Hosta* 'Halcyon' | Herbaceous Perennial |
| *Hymenocallis* × *festalis* | Bulb |
| *Ligularia* 'The Rocket' | Herbaceous Perennial |
| *Lilium martagon* 'Album' | Bulb |
| *Narcissus* 'Petrel' | Bulb |
| *Ornithogalum nutans* | Bulb |
| *Phlomis russeliana* | Herbaceous Perennial |
| *Phygelius* × *rectus* 'Moonraker' | Evergreen Shrub |
| *Phygelius* × *rectus* 'Winchester Fanfare' | Evergreen Shrub |
| *Sarcococca hookeriana* var. *digyna* 'Purple Stem' | Evergreen Shrub |
| *Sarcococca hookeriana* var. *humilis* | Evergreen Shrub |

## ARBORETUM

| | |
|---|---|
| *Acer japonicum* 'Aconitifolium' | Deciduous Tree |
| *Acer palmatum* 'Atropurpureum' | Deciduous Tree |
| *Acer palmatum* 'Bloodgood' | Deciduous Tree |
| *Acer palmatum* 'Butterfly' | Deciduous Tree |
| *Acer palmatum* 'Elegans' | Deciduous Tree |
| *Acer palmatum* 'Osakazuki' | Deciduous Tree |
| *Acer palmatum* 'Senkaki' | Deciduous Tree |
| *Acer palmatum* 'Shindeshōjō' | Deciduous Tree |
| *Acer palmatum* 'Sumi-nagashi' | Deciduous Tree |
| *Acer shirasawanum* 'Aureum' | Deciduous Tree |
| *Anemone nemorosa* | Herbaceous Perennial |
| Azalea *(Rhododendron)* 'Cannon's Double' | Deciduous Shrub |
| Azalea *(Rhododendron)* 'Fraseri' | Deciduous Shrub |
| Azalea *(Rhododendron)* 'Homebush' | Deciduous Shrub |
| Azalea *(Rhododendron)* 'Northern Hi-Lights' | Deciduous Shrub |
| Azalea *(Rhododendron) daviesii* | Deciduous Shrub |
| Azalea *(Rhododendron) luteum* | Deciduous Shrub |
| *Betula utilis* var. *jacquemontii* | Deciduous Tree |
| *Camellia* × *williamsii* 'Debbie' | Evergreen Shrub |
| *Cercidiphyllum japonicum* | Deciduous Tree |
| *Cercis siliquastrum* | Deciduous Tree |
| *Cornus* 'Norman Haddon' | Deciduous Shrub |
| *Cornus* 'Porlock' | Deciduous Shrub |
| *Cornus kousa* 'Milky Way' | Deciduous Shrub |
| *Cyclamen coum* | Bulb |
| *Cyclamen hederifolium* | Bulb |
| *Eranthus hyemalis* | Bulb |
| *Erythronium revolutum* 'Knightshayes Pink' | Bulb |
| *Galanthus nivalis* | Bulb |
| *Hyacinthoides non-scripta* | Bulb |
| *Hydrangea aspera* 'Macrophylla' | Deciduous Shrub |
| *Hydrangea aspera* subsp. *sargentiana* | Deciduous Shrub |
| *Hydrangea macrophylla* 'Ayesha' | Deciduous Shrub |
| *Hydrangea macrophylla* 'Dandenong' | Deciduous Shrub |
| *Hydrangea macrophylla* 'Fasan' | Deciduous Shrub |
| *Hydrangea macrophylla* 'Hamburg' | Deciduous Shrub |
| *Hydrangea macrophylla* 'Mrs W.J. Hepburn' | Deciduous Shrub |
| *Hydrangea macrophylla* 'Soeur Thérèse' | Deciduous Shrub |
| *Hydrangea macrophylla* 'Zorro' | Deciduous Shrub |
| *Hydrangea serrata* 'Tiara' | Deciduous Shrub |
| *Magnolia* 'Elizabeth' | Deciduous Tree |
| *Magnolia* 'Eskimo' | Deciduous Tree |
| *Magnolia* 'Gold Star' | Deciduous Tree |
| *Magnolia* 'Iolanthe' | Deciduous Tree |
| *Magnolia* 'Susan' | Deciduous Tree |
| *Magnolia* 'Trelissick Alba' | Deciduous Tree |
| *Magnolia dawsoniana* | Deciduous Tree |
| *Magnolia macrophylla* | Deciduous Tree |
| *Magnolia sinensis* | Deciduous Tree |
| *Magnolia soulangiana* 'Alba Superba' | Deciduous Tree |
| *Magnolia* Black Tulip | Deciduous Tree |
| *Magnolia* 'Caerhays Surprise' | Deciduous Tree |
| *Magnolia* × *procteriana* | Deciduous Tree |
| *Narcissus* 'Hawera' | Bulb |
| *Narcissus* 'Thalia' | Bulb |

| | |
|---|---|
| *Osmanthus serrulatus* | Evergreen Shrub |
| *Parrotia persica* | Deciduous Tree |
| *Prunus* 'Accolade' | Deciduous Tree |
| *Prunus sargentii* | Deciduous Tree |
| *Puschkinia libanotica* | Bulb |
| *Rhododendron* 'E.J.P Magor' | Evergreen Shrub |
| *Rhododendron arboreum* 'Tony Schilling' | Evergreen Shrub |
| *Rhododendron augustinii* | Evergreen Shrub |
| *Rhododendron* 'Loderi Fairyland' | Evergreen Shrub |
| *Rhododendron macabeanum* | Evergreen Shrub |
| *Rhododendron sino-falconeri* | Evergreen Shrub |
| *Rhododendron sinogrande* | Evergreen Shrub |
| *Rhododendron thompsonii* | Evergreen Shrub |
| *Scilla siberica* 'Spring Beauty' | Bulb |
| *Viburnum plicatum* 'Mariesii' | Deciduous Shrub |

## AZALEA WALK

| | |
|---|---|
| *Actinidia kolomikta* | Deciduous climber |
| *Asplenium scolopendrium* | Evergreen Fern |
| *Asplenium scolopendrium* 'Muricatum' | Evergreen Fern |
| *Athyrium filix-femina* | Deciduous Fern |
| Azalea *(Rhododendron)* 'Jolie Madame' | Deciduous Shrub |
| Azalea *(Rhododendron)* 'Nancy Waterer' | Deciduous Shrub |
| Azalea *(Rhododendron)* 'Northern Hi-Lights' | Deciduous Shrub |
| Azalea *(Rhododendron)* 'Princess Margaret of Windsor' | Deciduous Shrub |
| Azalea *(Rhododendron)* 'Raby' | Deciduous Shrub |
| Azalea *(Rhododendron)* 'Silver Slipper' | Deciduous Shrub |
| Azalea *(Rhododendron) luteum* | Deciduous Shrub |
| *Blechnum penna-marina* | Evergreen Fern |
| *Chaenomeles speciosa* 'Geisha Girl' | Deciduous Shrub |
| *Chaenomeles speciosa* 'Nivalis' | Deciduous Shrub |
| *Chaenomeles* × *superba* 'Cameo' | Deciduous Shrub |
| *Chaenomeles* × *superba* 'Jet Trail' | Deciduous Shrub |
| *Chionodoxa sardensis* | Bulb |
| *Clematis* 'Elizabeth' | Deciduous climber |
| *Clematis* 'Huldine' | Deciduous climber |
| *Clematis* Kingfisher | Deciduous climber |
| *Clematis montana* var. *rubens* | Deciduous climber |
| *Clematis* 'Mrs Cholmondeley' | Deciduous climber |
| *Dryopteris affinis* 'Cristata' (syn. 'The King') | Semi-evergreen Fern |
| *Dryopteris erythrosora* | Semi-evergreen Fern |
| *Dryopteris filix-mas* | Deciduous Fern |
| *Dryopteris filix-mas* 'Grandiceps Wills' | Deciduous Fern |
| *Dryopteris filix-mas* 'Revolvens' | Deciduous Fern |
| *Dryopteris wallichiana* | Semi-evergreen Fern |
| *Hedera colchica* | Evergreen Climber |
| *Hydrangea petiolaris* | Deciduous climber |
| *Parthenocissus henryana* | Deciduous climber |

## KITCHEN GARDEN

| | |
|---|---|
| Wall Fruit and Roses | Wall Fruit and Roses |
| Apricot 'Tomcot' | Deciduous Tree |
| Cherry 'Morello' | Deciduous Tree |
| Fig 'Brown Turkey' | Deciduous Tree |
| Gage 'Cambridge Gage' | Deciduous Tree |
| Gage 'Coe's Golden Drop' | Deciduous Tree |
| Gage 'Czar' | Deciduous Tree |
| Gage 'Green Gage' | Deciduous Tree |
| Gage 'Oullins Gage' | Deciduous Tree |
| Gooseberry 'Invicta' | Deciduous Shrub |
| Gooseberry 'Pax' | Deciduous Shrub |
| Pear 'Beth' | Deciduous Tree |
| Pear 'Beurré Hardy' | Deciduous Tree |
| Pear 'Conference' | Deciduous Tree |
| Pear 'Doyenné du Comice' | Deciduous Tree |
| Pear 'Williams' bon Chrétien' | Deciduous Tree |
| Plum 'Blue Tit' | Deciduous Tree |
| Plum 'Kirke's Blue' | Deciduous Tree |
| Plum 'Marjorie's Seedling' | Deciduous Tree |
| Plum 'Opal' | Deciduous Tree |
| Plum 'Swan' | Deciduous Tree |
| Redcurrant 'Red Lake' | Deciduous Shrub |
| *Rosa* 'Albertine' | Deciduous Climber |

| | |
|---|---|
| *Rosa* 'Cécille Brünner' | Deciduous Climber |
| | |
| *Espalier Apple Arches* | |
| Apple 'Egremont Russet' | Deciduous Tree |
| Apple 'Gloster '69' | Deciduous Tree |
| Apple 'Grenadier' | Deciduous Tree |
| Apple 'Lord Suffield' | Deciduous Tree |
| Apple 'Orleans Reinette' | Deciduous Tree |
| Apple 'Sturmer Pippin' | Deciduous Tree |
| | |
| *Full Standard Fruit Trees* | |
| Apple 'Ashmead's Kernel' | Deciduous Tree |
| Apple 'Beauty of Bath' | Deciduous Tree |
| Apple 'Discovery' | Deciduous Tree |
| Apple 'Egremont Russet' | Deciduous Tree |
| Apple 'Epicure' | Deciduous Tree |
| Apple 'Greensleeves' | Deciduous Tree |
| Apple 'Howgate Wonder' | Deciduous Tree |
| Apple 'James Grieve' | Deciduous Tree |
| Apple 'Lord Derby' | Deciduous Tree |
| Apple 'Newton Wonder' | Deciduous Tree |
| Apple 'Norfolk Beauty' | Deciduous Tree |
| Apple 'Orleans Reinette' | Deciduous Tree |
| Apple 'Reverend W. Wilks' | Deciduous Tree |
| Apple 'Rushcock Pearmain' | Deciduous Tree |
| Apple 'Spartan' | Deciduous Tree |
| Damson 'Merryweather' | Deciduous Tree |
| Pear 'Concorde' | Deciduous Tree |

CENTRAL HERB BEDS

| | |
|---|---|
| *Allium schoenoprasum* (Chives) | Herbaceous Perennial |
| *Angelica archangelica* | Biennial |
| *Delphinium* 'Blue Dawn' | Herbaceous Perennial |
| *Delphinium* 'Chelsea Star' | Herbaceous Perennial |
| *Delphinium* 'White Ruffles' | Herbaceous Perennial |
| *Hyssopus officinalis* | Evergreen Shrub |
| *Lavendula* 'Royal Purple' | Evergreen Shrub |
| *Mentha spicata* (Moroccan Mint) | Herbaceous Perennial |
| *Mentha spicata* (Spearmint) | Herbaceous Perennial |
| *Mentha suaveolens* (Applemint) | Herbaceous Perennial |
| *Mentha suaveolens* (Woolly Mint) | Herbaceous Perennial |
| *Origanum majorana* | Herbaceous Perennial |
| *Rosmarinus officinalis* | Evergreen Shrub |
| *Rosmarinus officinalis* 'Alba' | Evergreen Shrub |
| *Salvia officinalis* Broad-leaved form | Evergreen Shrub |
| *Thymus vulgaris* 'Compactus' | Evergreen Shrub |

BEHIND CENTRAL HERB BEDS

| | |
|---|---|
| *Malus × zumi* 'Golden Hornet' | Deciduous Tree |
| *Rosmarinus* 'Miss Jessopp's Upright' | Evergreen Shrub |

CENTRAL HERBACEOUS BORDERS

| | |
|---|---|
| *Actaea simplex* 'Pink Spike' | Herbaceous Perennial |
| *Agapanthus* 'Cobolt Blue' | Herbaceous Perennial |
| *Allium christophii* | Bulb |
| *Anemone × hybrida* 'Königin Charlotte' | Herbaceous Perennial |
| *Aquilegia* 'Blue Star' | Herbaceous Perennial |
| *Aquilegia* 'Clemantine Rose' | Herbaceous Perennial |
| *Aster cordifolius* 'Little Carlow' | Herbaceous Perennial |
| *Aster novi-belgii* 'Blue Lagoon' | Herbaceous Perennial |
| *Astrantia major* 'Buckland' | Herbaceous Perennial |
| *Delphinium* 'Blue Dawn' | Herbaceous Perennial |
| *Delphinium* 'Chelsea Star' | Herbaceous Perennial |
| *Delphinium* 'White Ruffles' | Herbaceous Perennial |
| *Campanula latifolia* blue-flowered | Herbaceous Perennial |
| *Echinacea* 'Bressingham hybrids' | Herbaceous Perennial |
| *Geranium* Rozanne (syn. 'Jolly Bee') | Herbaceous Perennial |
| *Geranium psilostemon* | Herbaceous Perennial |
| *Iris* 'Caesar's Brother' | Herbaceous Perennial |
| *Narcissus triandrus* 'Cheerfulness' | Bulb |
| *Narcissus triandrus* 'Yellow Cheerfulness' | Bulb |
| *Philadelphus corinarius* 'Aureus' | Deciduous Shrub |

| | |
|---|---|
| *Phlox carolina* 'Bill Baker' | Herbaceous Perennial |
| *Phlox paniculata* 'Miss Ellie' | Herbaceous Perennial |
| *Salvia nemorosa* 'Caradonna' | Herbaceous Perennial |
| *Sedum* Herbstfreude Group | Herbaceous Perennial |

OUTSIDE BORDERS

| | |
|---|---|
| *Akebia quinata* 'Alba' | Semi-evergreen Climber |
| *Anthemis tinctoria* 'E.C Buxton' | Herbaceous Perennial |
| *Artemesia* 'Oriental Limelight' | Evergreen Shrub |
| *Brachyglottis* (syn. *Senecio*) 'Sunshine' | Evergreen Shrub |
| *Chimnanthus praecox* | Deciduous Shrub |
| *Cistus pulverulentus* 'Sunset' | Evergreen Shrub |
| *Cistus × purpureus* | Evergreen Shrub |
| *Clematis* 'Purpurea Plena' | Deciduous Climber |
| *Dahlia merkii* | Herbaceous Perennial |
| *Dianthus* 'Devon Wizard' | Evergreen Perennial |
| *Eucommis bicolor* | Bulb |
| *Foeniculum vulgare* 'Purpureum' | Herbaceous Perennial |
| *Fragaria vesca* | Evergreen Perennial |
| *Geranium clarkei* 'Kashmir White' | Herbaceous Perennial |
| *Geranium × oxonianum* 'Claridge Druce' | Herbaceous Perennial |
| *Gladiolus nanus* 'Nathalie' | Bulb |
| *Gladiolus × colvillii* | Bulb |
| *Helleborus argutifolius* | Evergreen Perennial |
| *Jasminum fruiticans* | Semi-evergreen Shrub |
| *Lilium* 'African Queen' | Bulb |
| *Lilium henryi* | Bulb |
| *Narcissus* 'W.P Milner' | Bulb |
| *Penstemon* 'Port Wine' | Herbaceous Perennial |
| *Phlomis fruiticosa* | Evergreen Shrub |
| *Phlomis longifolia* | Evergreen Shrub |
| *Rosmarinus officinalis* | Evergreen Shrub |
| *Salvia patens* 'Guanajuato' | Herbaceous Perennial |
| *Sedum spectable* 'Autumn Joy' | Herbaceous Perennial |
| *Spirea japonica* 'Goldflame' | Deciduous Shrub |

DOMES

| | |
|---|---|
| *Clematis* 'Hagley Hybrid' | Deciduous Climber |
| *Clematis* 'John Warren' | Deciduous Climber |
| *Clematis montana* var. *grandiflora* | Deciduous Climber |
| *Clematis montana* var. *wilsonii* | Deciduous Climber |
| *Clematis* 'Princess Diana' | Deciduous Climber |
| *Clematis* 'Alba Luxurians' | Deciduous Climber |
| *Lonicera periclymenum* 'Belgica' | Deciduous Climber |
| *Rosa* 'Francis E. Lester' | Deciduous Climber |
| *Rosa* 'Paul's Himalayan Musk' | Deciduous Climber |
| *Wisteria sinensis* | Deciduous Climber |

EDGING PATHS, BEDS AND BORDERS

| | |
|---|---|
| *Helleborus orientalis* | Evergreen Perennial |
| *Rosa mundi* (syn. *R. gallica* 'Versicolor') | Deciduous shrub. |
| *Rosa rubiginosa* | Deciduous shrub. |
| *Teucrium × lucidrys* | Evergreen Shrub |

# SUPPLIERS AND CONTRIBUTORS

Julian and Isabel Bannerman: Trematon Castle, Saltash, Cornwall PL12 4QW

William Bertram: The Studio, Woodrising, Timsbury, Bath BA2 0EU; 01761 471100

David Blisset Ph.D, RIBA, Chartered Architect: Ashbrook, Amport, Hampshire SP11 8BE; 01264 771768

Emma Clark, Islamic Garden Design: www.emma-clark.com

Richard Craven: Jack Clee's, North Sutton, Stanton Lacey, Ludlow, Shropshire SY8 2AJ

Nick Dunn (Fruit expert) Frank P Matthews Ltd: Berrington Couret, Tenbury Wells, Worcestershire WR15; 01584 810214; www.frankpmatthews.com

Simon Fairlie, Austrian Scythes: Monkton Wyld Court, Charmouth, Bridport, Dorset DT6 6DQ; www.thescytheshop.co.uk

Stephen Florence (Furniture maker and designer): Y Gorlan, Pentre Farm, Llanfair Clydogau, SA48 8LE; 07557 519242; www.stephenflorence.com

John Hill (Planting): Sherborne Gardens, Sherborne, Glos. GL54 3DW; 01451 844522

Jekka McVicar, Jekka's Herb Farm: Rose Cottage, Shellards Lane, Alveston, Bristol BS35 3SY; 01454 418878; www.jekkasherbfarm.com

Charles Morris LVO, FRICS: The Green, Priory Road. Blythburgh, Suffolk IP19 9LR; 01502 478493

Jonathan Myles-Lea (Illustrator): The Folly, Laskett Gardens, Much Birch, Herefordshire HR2 8HZ; 00132 32831028; www.myles-lea.com

David Nash, c/o Annely Juda Fine Art: 23 Dering Street, London W1S 1AW; 02076 297578

Geoffrey Preston (Sculptor): Eagle Yard, Tudor Street, Exeter EX4 3BR; 01392 423263; www.geoffreypreston.co.uk

William Pye: 31 Bellevue Road, London SW17 7EF; 02086 82 2727; www.williampye.com

Will Sibley (Fruit expert): East Malling Trust, Bradbourne House, East Malling, Kent, ME19 6DZ

Sir Roy Strong (Topiary design): The Laskett, Much Birch, Herefordshire, HR2 8HZ

John White (Arboretum design): Redvers, Bodenham, Hereford, HR1 3HR; 01568 797222

Winterborne Zelston Fencing Ltd: Blandford Forum, Dorset, DT11 9EU; 01929 459245

# ACKNOWLEDGEMENTS

This book has been compiled with the help of many different people but, first and foremost, huge thanks are due to Bunny Guinness for her immense patience and effort. Deserving equal thanks are the gardeners and staff at Highgrove – especially Head Gardener, Debs Goodenough, and Deputy Head Gardener, John Ridgley – Ed Bollom, Fred Ind, Paul Duckett, Steve Staines, Dennis Brown, Marion Cox and Rebecca Casewell for their collective efforts in maintaining this remarkable garden. The garden guides also contributed much valuable history and insight, especially Shane Hoskins, Georgie Barnard and Amanda Hornby.

In addition, special thanks are due to the many people who helped to create the garden and gave a lot of their time, including Mollie, Lady Salisbury, Dame Miriam Rothschild, Willie Bertram, Julian and Isabel Bannerman, David Blissett, Sir Roy Strong, Charles Morris, Rosemary Verey, Vernon Russell-Smith, Gary Mantle, Emma Clark, Richard Craven, Nick Dunn, Jekka McVicar, Stephen Florence, John Hill, David Nash, William Pye, Mark Hoare, Will Sibley and John White.

Kristina Kyriacou, from the office of Their Royal Highnesses The Prince of Wales and The Duchess of Cornwall, project managed the entire process and provided invaluable help and support.

Integral to proceedings, and therefore also deserving of recognition, are Lord Weidenfeld, Amanda Harris, Jillian Young, Clare Hennessy, Lucie Stericker and all at Orion; Pat Lomax and Christine Prescott of Highgrove Enterprises.

Last, but not least, Bunny Guinness would like to thank Sophia Graham, Barbara Stockitt and Kevin Guinness for their help, patience and support.

# INDEX

First published in Great Britain in 2014
by Weidenfeld & Nicolson,
an imprint of The Orion Publishing Group Ltd

1 3 5 7 9 10 8 6 4 2

Orion House
Upper St Martin's Lane
London WC2H 9EA
An Hachette UK Company

PHOTOGRAPHY Marianne Majerus, Andrew Butler
and Andrew Lawson
DESIGNER Philip Lewis
ILLUSTRATOR Carolyn Jenkins
PROJECT EDITOR Jillian Young
COPY EDITOR Helena Caldon
PROOFREADER Diana Vowles
INDEXER Judith Menes

A CIP catalogue record for this book is available
from the British Library.

ISBN 978-0-297-86935-1

Printed and bound in Italy by Printer Trento S.r.l.

MIX
Paper from
responsible sources
FSC® C015829
www.fsc.org

www.orionbooks.co.uk

PAGE ONE A window in one of the pepperpot buildings
on the Terrace.
PAGE TWO *Campanula lactiflora* 'Prichard's Variety' is
featured in the Sundial Garden.
PAGE THREE The view of the Kitchen Garden from the
Azalea Walk.
PAGE FOUR His Royal Highness surrounded by June blooms
in the Mediterranean Garden.
PAGE FIVE The parallel borders in the Kitchen Garden have
large clusters of delphiniums, one of The Prince's favourites.
RIGHT One of the rose arbours in the Kitchen Garden in Summer.

*Highgrove House*

*Orchard Room*

South Front & Sundial Garden

*Dovecote*

*Sanctuary*

*The Golden Column*

1   Orchard Room
2   Garden Entrance
3   Buttress Garden
4   Laurel Tunnel
5   Borghese Gladiator
6   Lily Pool Garden
7   Lime Avenue
8   Dovecote
9   Wild Flower Meadow
10  Boundary of Stumpery including:
11  Temple of Worthies
12  Wall of Gifts
13  Japanese Moss Garden
14  Tree House
15  Temples
16  End of Stumpery
17  Lower Orchard
18  Winterbourne Garden
19  Kitchen Garden
20  Azalea Walk
21  Arboretum
22  Daughters of Odessa
23  Sanctuary
24  Front Drive
25  Avenue
26  Front of House
27  Sundial Garden
28  Terrace Garden
29  Thyme Walk
30  Oak Pavilion
31  Acid Bed
32  Rose Pergola
33  Cottage Garden
34  Carpet Garden

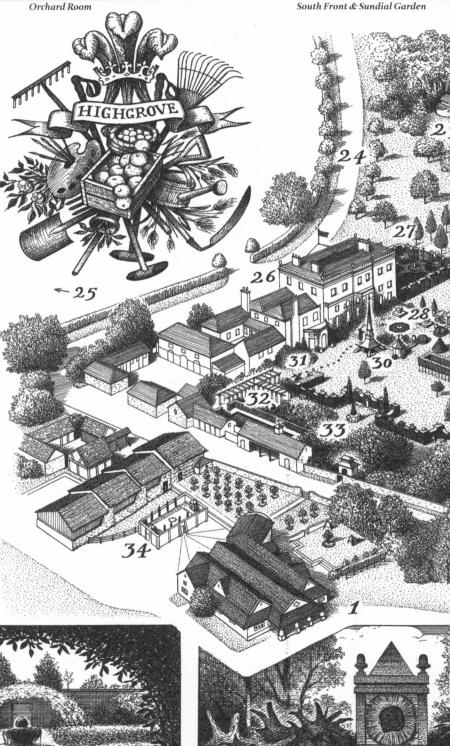

*Kitchen Garden*

*Temple of Worthies*